Love
Bishop

J~~~~

BABY,
YOU ARE SO FINE

• WHAT WOMEN NEED •

• WHAT MEN WANT •

BY BISHOP DENNIS LEONARD

Published in Denver, Colorado, by Dennis Leonard
Publishing
ISBN 1-880809-07-9

Printed In The United States of America

CONTENTS

DEDICATION

I dedicate this book to my wonderful wife, Michele. She is truly the helper in my life that encourages and inspires me to be all that I can be. She is a praying woman who always has my back covered and is such a strength for me. Thank you, Michele, for all of your love, dedication and hard work. Baby, you are so fine!

And, to my two sons, Mark and Garret; You have brought such joy to my life. You are both very gifted and talented men and I thank God that you have dedicated your lives and talents to the Lord. You are both great leaders and I am very proud of you. Your greatest days are still ahead.

FOREWORD

From the beginning of time, God put "the family" at the top of His agenda. When He created Adam & Eve, it was all about family and relationships. So naturally, that which God has invested the most in and desires us to do the same, the devil attacks the most. The devil is out to destroy the family.

But in the midst of the destruction, God has raised up a man of God namely, Bishop Dennis Leonard, to deal with the issues surrounding the family and relationships.

In this powerful book, Bishop Leonard gives us the key to getting the family on the right track and some necessary guidelines to keep them there. When someone offers to me keys to success or guidelines on how to succeed, I prefer that it is a person that has "gone through" that is to say, has experienced some things in this area. "An ounce of experience is worth more than a thousand words." A testimony only comes from a test.

Bishop Leonard faced great difficulty in his personal life, but to see how he has gone through it all and come out says to me that he is indeed the man to write this book. Knowing him personally, I admire the powerful relationship between he and his family.

He is a great role model for the world today, especially when so many people are giving up. As busy as he is, (serving as pastor of one of America's greatest churches and one of the most sought after evangelists in our world today), quality time with his family is at the top of his agenda. Bishop Leonard, having a great relationship with his wife and family, is the kind of person we need to hear from.

Over the years, this great man of God has observed carefully, the family and relationships. Also, he has mastered the art of listening. "Knowledge speaks and wisdom listens." Consequently he has developed a real sensitivity to families and what they go through. Now that he has observed and listened, he is now ready to speak to us, what he knows and what God has given to him. His message has worked in his home. His message has worked in his church. Now he shares it with us, the world.

If your family is torn apart, this book is for you. If you need a "tune-up" to keep your relationship running smoothly, this book is for you. Family means relationship. Relationship means responsibility. I believe when each of us take responsibility for our ability (that which we are able to do), the family will be stronger and relationships will be better.

Bishop Paul S. Morton, Sr.
International Presiding Bishop
Full Gospel Baptist Church Fellowship

XII

INTRODUCTION

Men and women have different needs and wants and those differences are magnified in marriage. Many marriages today have been destroyed because of a lack of love and a lack of communication.

What has happened between your wedding day and where you are today? What has caused the two of you to be at each other's throats, or caused you to not trust each other?

There was a day when you couldn't live without each other and today you are having trouble imagining one more day together.

Marriage is not easy. It requires hard work in order to make it succeed. The information contained in this book will help you to; better understand your mate's needs...learn how to put the past behind you and move forward...make a difference in your children's lives...and finally, make a difference in your life.

1

PERSONAL RELATIONSHIPS

We live in a high tech, low touch society. In some ways it is easier to get through life learning and knowing instead of loving and feeling. However, God made us to be creatures with strong emotions. We want to touch, and we need to be touched.

Another characteristic of our society is that we are constantly stimulated with sexual images, suggestive speech, and sexual temptation and yet we don't know how to create lasting relationships that remain strong no matter what life brings our way. We know every possible way to make love, yet we have no idea how to love. The Bible says that in the last days there would be perilous times. Let me tell you, perilous times are definitely upon us.

The number one problem that Christians face today has to do with the family. The school systems do not support parents, Hollywood has done everything possible to erode family values, and divorce is everywhere.

> *Many people today do not know how to share themselves and build great personal relationships...*

Many people today do not know how to share themselves and build great personal relationships simply because their past experiences have shown them that when you share yourself, you get burned.

So we become more and more self-centered in order to survive. When you add to this mix the twist sex brings, you have people who have given their bodies and hearts away so many times that they are totally empty and have no more heart or self to give.

Paul told Timothy that in the last days, people would become more and more self-centered, and Jesus said that in the last days, people's love for each other would grow colder and colder. Because the sin nature is self-centered, we want to know what we can get out of a relationship rather than what we can contribute to it. However, when our pasts are so tangled and our hearts so empty, we are incapable of loving. A touch from Jesus is the only way to bring true change.

We have a spiritual enemy that does everything possible to break up relationships. Jesus said a house divided cannot stand, and that's why the enemy is always trying to divide. When we have healthy relationships, we are stronger.

The enemy is always trying to separate people so he can weaken them. He loves to attack Christian marriages in order to cripple the family.

It is God's desire in a marriage covenant for both partners to be unselfish and giving. Ladies listen, you'll never motivate your man by nagging him. But you can motivate him by honoring him. You can motivate him by supporting him and letting him know that he is your "Knight in Shining Armor."

> *The marriage covenant means, "I've got you, babe." It means that my strengths are now yours and your strengths are now mine.*

The marriage covenant means, "I've got you, babe." It means that my strengths are now yours and your strengths are now mine. It means that we are in this thing together, come hell or high water. It means that together we are one, and we can fight anything and win.

You know that a relationship is healthy when both sides feel love and support. If you are in a dating relationship and don't feel this love and support, you need to seriously reconsider the relationship.

We are all insecure by nature. That's why we need the love and support of those around us.

> ...how your spiritual enemy loves it when you fall out with others. That's because his plan is to divide and conquer...

No man is an island and God made us in such a way that we need others. We must learn the importance of healthy teamwork.

The marriage covenant means that no matter what happens, I'll be there for you and you'll be there for me. We will be so strong together that we can disagree on issues but still support each other in principle.

Oh, how your spiritual enemy loves it when you fall out with others. That's because his plan is to divide and conquer, then weaken you through broken relationships. So your fighting and disagreeing is only making his job easier.

Anytime people think you are unhappy with them, they will feel insecure. If your wife feels you don't care about her and have no plans to defend her, it's only a matter of time until she finds someone who will care. If you make your husband feel as though he doesn't make enough money, you are attacking his manhood. If you disrespect him enough, he will explode, or more often than not, he will quietly walk away.

Anytime two people are married and they live totally separate lives, they are in danger of becoming roommates instead of help-mates. Anytime a married couple takes separate vacations and have separate bank accounts, you can bet that they are not one flesh. It is God's desire that the two of you give up your selfish dreams and build dreams together.

> *Anytime two people are married and they live totally separate lives, they are in danger of becoming roommates instead of helpmates.*

As Christians, we must have a strong commitment to the Lord above everything else. This is so important because there will come a time when a spouse will hurt you and you will feel like walking away. If your commitment is to the Lord, you can weather every storm. Mature love is committed to the Lord first and then to each other. This is the very reason that shacking up never works; the commitment level is not the same.

So many people think that marriage solves the loneliness problem. But unless there is strong commitment, marriage doesn't solve loneliness. Unless there is proper communication, love and support, you can be married and be lonely. In fact, marriage will reveal the excess baggage you are both carrying. Because of the intimacy in marriage, living in the same house will expose all your weaknesses.

Ladies, if you have a problem with men in general, marriage will expose it. If anyone has an insecurity problem, it will definitely come out in marriage.

Men, if you have a jealously problem, marriage will cause it to manifest itself very quickly. Marriage tends to put a spotlight on your weaknesses and will magnify your problem areas quite soon.

> It's interesting that when you date, you are drawn to each other's strengths. But after you're married for a while, those same strengths can drive you up the wall.

We all enter marriage thinking that our partner and this covenant will solve our problems. After you are married for a while, every weakness becomes obvious in both you and your spouse. All the little quirks you thought were so cute before marriage may become thorns in your flesh.

It's interesting that when you date, you are drawn to each other's strengths. But after you're married for a while, those same strengths can drive you up the wall.

While we're dating, we seem to hide our weaknesses pretty well, but after a while, the real you is revealed – the true you shows up. That's because as time passes, you lower your guard and unresolved issues spring out and pride peeps through. Then, lo and behold, your excess baggage becomes evident.

That's why you must date and know someone for a period of time, so that you can determine what their weaknesses are and whether or not you can accept those weaknesses, and vice versa.

We try so hard to change the people around us, but the truth of the matter is that you can't change anybody. You can't even change yourself without God's help, and you certainly can't change your mate. Partly that's because men and women are so different in relationships. We think differently. We respond differently. We see things from a totally different perspective.

> *We try so hard to change the people around us, but the truth of the matter is that you can't change anybody. You can't even change yourself...*

Men seem to be insensitive, while women seem to be overly sensitive. Men are goal oriented, while women tend to be relationship oriented. Men have a conquering attitude, while women wonder why men act so macho.

God told the man to subdue the earth and rule over every living thing. That's why a man will get up early in the morning to go fishing and not even like fish. It's all a part of him conquering and subduing.

When a man is in the corporate world, he sees himself as subduing and conquering. He is conquering that business deal.

When a man gets behind the wheel of a car, he is conquering the road. That's why he gets so upset when somebody pulls in front of him. In his mind someone is violating his rights. Someone is trying to stop him from conquering.

If you go on a trip with a man behind the wheel of a car, he is like "pac-man." He is trying to eat up the road, one mile at a time. The reason he doesn't want to stop and let you go to the bathroom is because he is afraid someone is going to get in front of him.

God told the man to subdue the earth and rule over every living thing. That's why a man will get up early in the morning to go fishing and not even like fish.

Men and women are very different when it comes to shopping! A woman can go from shop to shop. She can try on twelve different outfits and not buy one thing. But a man shops the way he drives. He knows where he wants to go, and he takes the shortest route there. He goes to one store, gets what he wants and then leaves. He has reached his goal. He has conquered. He has killed his prey. He has thrown his prey over his shoulder and gone home.

One reason a woman can be unhappy in a marriage is because the man stops pursuing her. In other words, if a man is not careful, he will communicate that he feels he has conquered his wife and stop giving her that special attention he used to give. This lack of special attention makes her feel as though she is being ignored.

This is another example of why we need to learn to listen to each other properly. If we would listen carefully, we wouldn't have these misunderstandings because we would be in tune with each other.

We must learn to give to each other unselfishly, so that the problems in our marriages are solved before they get too big. God's plan is for the husband to be so giving to his wife that she cannot resist his love and for the wife to be so giving to her husband that he cannot resist her love.

> *One reason a woman can be unhappy in a marriage is because the man stops pursuing her. In other words, if a man is not careful, he will communicate that he feels he has conquered his wife...*

Paul said that husbands ought to love their wives as their own bodies. The man who loves his wife, loves himself. If you love and give to your spouse, then you are loving and giving to yourself.

That's why couples need to make all major decisions together. If you do not include your spouse in the decision-making process, it makes him or her feel unloved and insecure.

We all hear love differently. Men need to be admired and respected. They need physical pleasure. Women need to be told they are loved and need emotional support.

When a woman denies her husband physical pleasure, he can believe the romance is dead and start looking for it elsewhere.

> *If you do not include your spouse in the decision-making process, it makes him or her feel unloved and insecure.*

When a wife isn't told how much she is loved and appreciated, she too can start looking elsewhere for romance. Both of them must understand the different needs men and women have and work on meeting those needs.

Sex in a marriage is very important. I will even go so far as to say that if you have a good sexual relationship in your marriage, you are probably more stable. There is something about sexual frustration that leads to bitterness and hostility. Anytime you refuse to meet the sexual needs of your spouse, you can bet that great resentment and tension will build.

How do you hear love? It is important to figure out the answer to this question so you can communicate your needs to your loved ones, especially to your spouse. Some people need a phone call in the middle of the day. Some need to hear, "I love you."

The Apostle Paul said women need to be told all the time

they are loved. Men think that translates to once a month or at most, once a week. No, tell her as often as she needs to hear it, and this is over and over and over again.

Some people need to be admired more than others. Some people need to be touched continually. Some people need to be told they are wonderful and encouraged a great deal. How do you hear love?

When a marriage is in trouble, it's because someone's needs are not being met. When a marriage is in trouble, it's because someone is not listening or not paying attention. When a marriage is in trouble, it's because someone is not being supported or loved properly.

> *When a marriage is in trouble, it's because someone's needs are not being met. When a marriage is in trouble, it's because someone is not listening or not paying attention.*

If you want to have a great relationship, sit down and talk with the person you wish to have this great relationship with, and find out how they hear love. Find out how you can support them in a better way. Find out how you can meet their needs.

One mistake many couples make today is that they become sexually involved before they become best friends. Once sex enters into a relationship, you don't work on personal issues the same way. That's why the Word tells us not to have sex before marriage.

If you are married to your best friend, you can weather every storm that comes your way. If you are married to your best friend, you can talk about anything and solve your problems. If you're currently married to someone who is not your best friend, you need to start building each other up, and giving in an unselfish way.

> *If you are married to your best friend, you can weather every storm that comes your way. If you are married to your best friend, you can talk about anything...*

If you'll speak the right kinds of words to your spouse, he or she will not be looking for approval from someone at work. Even if things aren't going well in your relationship, learn to bless and curse not.

If you're going to see healing, there are some things you have to let go. Some things aren't worth hanging on to. If you're going to see healing in your life, you have to say, "What's done is done, but from this day forward I am going to make some changes."

2

BABY, YOU ARE SO FINE

Whether you are single or married, you need to realize that there are numerous differences between men and women. We feel things differently, we think differently, and we respond differently. God made us to be different for a variety of reasons. He created the man to be the provider for the family, to lead the family, and to protect the family. God put the man in the garden, and He told him to dress it and to work it (Gen. 2:15). From the very beginning, God assigned a job to every man. Also from the very beginning, He established the man as the head of the home.

There is a tendency to think that relationships were introduced in the Bible with Adam and Eve. However, relationships were introduced into the creation story when God said, *"Let us create man in our own image and in our likeness" (Gen. 1:26).*

Some Old Testament scholars maintain that the Hebrew construction of this sentence makes it very clear that God is relationally interacting with Himself. That is, the Father, the Son, and the Holy Spirit, as one, agreed together that mankind needed the same type of close interaction experienced in the Godhead.

> *"For this reason a man will leave his father and mother and be united with his wife, and the two will become one flesh" (Gen. 2:24).*

God has three distinct parts, or persons, but is one God. Each one of these parts has a specific role, and yet none of the three is greater or lesser than the other. God desires this same type of functional design between the man and woman: functionally different and yet equal.

This personifies what God meant after He brought Adam and Eve together: "For this reason a man will leave his father and mother and be united with his wife, and the two will become one flesh" (Gen. 2:24). Marriage was designed to create "one flesh" out of two individuals. Just as the three persons of the Godhead are one, so should the partners in a marriage be one.

God Has Designed An Order

God designed the man to work and to lead his family, and He designed the woman to adapt to the man. I am not suggesting that women are not capable of leading because they are, but God made the man to be the decision-maker and the woman to support him. Anytime a woman has to lead a family, even if she has strong leadership abilities, there will be difficulties because that's not the *role* that God designed for women. God did not design the woman to provide for her family. When a married woman is the breadwinner she is out of place.

> *Just as the three persons of the Godhead are one, so should the partners in a covenant marriage be one.*

And ladies, may I suggest to you that if you have your eye on a man who won't work and feels that working and providing is solely your role, not only is that man out of God's order, but that man is not good enough for you! If the man that you are interested in is looking for a job, then you need to wait and see what he's going to do.

You need to wait to see if he's going to be a proper provider for your future and the future of your family. You need to ask yourself and evaluate, "Does this man set the example that I want to put before my children?" You need to wait to see if he's going to accomplish what he says he is going to do. Is he a man of his word or is he just "playing you" until he gets what he wants?

> *Is the man you are dating a man of his word or is he just "playing you" until he gets what he wants?*

If a man is not working, then he's not fulfilling his purpose as a man. These are all significant reasons why you should not create a sexual bond or "soul tie" with a man outside of marriage. Don't sacrifice your entire future on a man that is not good enough for you.

God designed the woman to be the primary care-giver and source of nurture for small children. Make no mistake here, men are to also nurture and care for their children, but we're speaking of God's design. Men are the *primary* protectors and providers, and women the *primary* nurturers and care-givers. But, because of the socio-economics of today's society, many wives are forced to work outside of the home.

As a result, many of today's children are being reared by daycare providers, yet we appear surprised when some of these children do the things they do and act the way they act. Some parents must look at their children in shock and realize that they really don't even know them.

I know that every situation is different, but if there is any way to keep your children out of daycare, they will be better off. God meant parents to care for their own children if at all possible.

When the woman is out of her role as the mother and wife in the home, she can become frustrated and the children may become rebellious. If you want to see a frustrated woman, then make her the breadwinner in the family. If you want to see a frustrated woman, then make her take the lead of the house and put all of the responsibility of the bills and the children on her.

> *As men of God, we need to do everything that we can to keep the woman in the role that God designed for her.*

As men of God, we need to do everything that we can to keep the woman in the role that God designed for her. Please don't misunderstand me here. Some women enjoy working, and it doesn't affect their role at home at all. If that's truly the case, fine. But men, don't force your wives to work if it isn't necessary. Having a happy home is more important than having a few extra bucks. And men, when you keep your wife happy, she'll make sure you're kept happy!

Because the wife is the help-meet to the husband, she needs her man to take the lead. He needs to take the initiative and with his wife's input, present a vision for the household. Having done this, he needs to consistently show ownership of the plan and persist in seeing that it is carried through to completion.

The wife needs for her man to take charge and say, at least in effect, "Remember, this is the plan for our family, and this is how we are going to do it." But wives, when your husband has presented a plan, don't go behind his back and work against it. If you are going to allow him to lead, then let him lead. This won't be easy at times, but it's important.

MEN NEED WOMEN'S HELP

God made the man to be the leader of the family and to guide the family to successful solutions to problems that arise. Men, by nature, try to find out what is wrong and then go to work correcting it, so they are usually good at evaluating problems and devising solutions. On the other hand, men tend to want problems "fixed" immediately and are often too direct. They need the natural nurturing qualities of a woman to bring them in balance.

Without this balance, men can easily become abrasive and/ or assume the posture of the lecturer – ready at the drop of a hat to give a remedy for every dilemma or an opinion on whatever subject is at hand. One simple method for men to be less abrasive is to listen, really listen, more and pontificate less. I said this was simple, I didn't say it was easy.

Focused listening also helps the speaker to feel "heard" and cared for and keeps the listener from being perceived as a shallow, abrupt answer man. Women are generally better listeners and instinctively tend to bring a healing touch to relationships. Men need to appreciate what women bring to relationships and let the woman in their lives help them.

God made men to lead, to cultivate the garden, to instruct, to guide, and to be problem-solvers. Because men are problem-solvers, they have a tendency to do things rather than communicate about them. Women, on the other hand, are much more social and tend to communicate about things rather than do them.

One simple method for men to be less abrasive is to listen, really listen, more and pontificate less. I said this was simple, I didn't say it was easy.

If a man is not careful, he can wound his wife's spirit in the way he communicates with her. If a woman discloses certain things important in her life, her husband may cut her off and not listen because he is a bottom-line person. Men like to fix things, but they do not want to discuss things. However, sometimes women do not want everything fixed. Sometimes a woman just wants her man to sit down and listen.

This may not be easy for a man to do because he wants to hear the bottom line. Yet a woman feels loved when her husband will take the time to listen and not cut her off when she's talking by interjecting a quick solution to "solve the problem." He must resist the impulse to treat her concerns as items of business that need to be moved through until they are all checked off or solved.

The woman is to support her husband and be an advisor to him. Since she is good at communication she will talk to her man to try to improve him. But, if she is not careful it will sound like nagging. God commands the woman to honor and to respect her husband (Eph. 5:33). Women, therefore, should be very careful about the way they talk to their husbands. A woman may think that she is building up her husband by continually reminding him to take care of business or by always correcting him. But her efforts may sound like nagging or even belittle him and actually create the opposite effect and cause her husband to feel a lack of respect.

Men like to fix things, but they do not want to talk. However, sometimes women do not want everything fixed. Sometimes a woman just wants her man to sit down and listen.

Because the man is goal and task oriented he draws his self-esteem from accomplishing goals. He is competitive, takes such pride in his job and his things, and seems to be very pushy at times. This is why he wants to excel on his job; he feels as though he is conquering and winning at the same time.

YOU MUST BE FRIENDS FIRST

When you see a woman who looks unhappy, it can generally be traced back to an abusive father or an abusive husband. Many times it can be traced to a man who took advantage of her, or mistreated her in some way, or did not talk to her properly. Men must be careful how they talk to their wives. A man will raise his voice sometimes and not realize that he has raised it. When a man does this, the woman should not yell back at him, but nicely tell him that he is yelling at her. Many times he may not realize how sensitive his wife is to a raised voice.

> *Because the man is goal-oriented and task-oriented, he draws his self-esteem from accomplishing goals.*

And ladies, if you are single, it is important for you to choose a man who will nourish you, who will cherish you, and who will talk to you properly. It is important that when you meet someone you do not get emotionally involved with that person until you know what the real person is actually like.

God commanded the man to love, to cherish, and to nourish his wife (Eph. 5:29). He didn't command wives to love their husbands because God knew that women do not have a problem with these things. They do not have a problem showing love, but men usually have to work at it.

In the dating process, it is important that you look at the things a person has to offer. Do they add to you emotionally? Do they have the same desires as you? Are their goals the same as yours? What is their walk with the Lord really like? You can both be Christians and still be unequally yoked. And, just because you meet someone in church, doesn't mean that this is the person for you.

> *God commanded the man to love, to cherish, and to nourish his wife (Eph. 5:29).*

Now that you are born again it is important that you do not get emotionally involved with someone until there is a mutual commitment, a mutual love, and a mutual respect for each other. It is important that when you meet someone you keep your distance for an appropriate length of time.

You have to take time to be friends and to get to know each other. And, ladies, this is why you must be very careful about the way that you dress. Men are very visual and very sexual in the way they think. If you try to entice him with your body, then that is all you will ever have in your relationship.

Marriage is not so much about finding the one right person for you, it is about having common interests and about building a life together. It is about being committed to each other's needs, about supporting each other's goals and dreams. If you cannot support each other when you are single, then you will not support each other after you are married.

CULTIVATE YOUR GARDEN PROPERLY

God said He created the man to cultivate the garden. Yes, God created man to work, but the man is supposed to bring out the best in the garden. This means the man is supposed to bring out the best in his wife and children. If the husband nourishes and encourages his wife properly, then she will grow emotionally and spiritually. But, if he is not careful and does not say the right things, then he can hurt her or damage her.

If a man is cultivating his own garden properly, then his wife will maintain her beauty. If a husband is nourishing his wife properly, then people will know that she has a good man. Men, if your wife does not look better after you marry her, then you are doing something wrong. Your wife is a product of the way you care for her and nurture her.

God made the man to be a giver and the woman to be a receiver. If you are giving proper attention to your wife, then she will grow and be a happy woman. If you are not giving her proper attention, then there will be problems. A woman will fall deeply in love with a man who will give her attention and listen to her. Remember, men are goal-oriented so they are not good listeners naturally, but a smart man will slow down and learn to listen.

The Bible says, "He who finds a wife finds a good thing, and obtains favor from the Lord" (Prov. 18:22). Men, one of the reasons God brought you a wife was to bring something good into your life. If you are encouraging your wife properly, she will believe she is a good thing and will rise to the occasion. If you continually call her a good thing in your life, then she will feel loved and she will respond accordingly.

> Men, if your wife does not look better after you marry her, then you are doing something wrong. Your wife is a product of the way you care for her and nurture her.

BEING ALONE IS NOT GOOD

Let's go back to the Garden of Eden where God said, "It is not good that the man should be alone" (Gen. 2:18). He knew that men do not communicate well and need someone around them to help. Whether we are male or female, we all need relationships in our lives or we will struggle. The problem with men is that they do not realize how much they need relationships.

God did not say it was not good to be *single*. He said it was not good to be *alone*. There is a big difference between these two because you can be single and not be lonely. If you suffer from loneliness, it is not because you are single, but because you are all alone and do not have proper relationships. You must learn how to communicate and build relationships if you are going to overcome loneliness.

If you are married and your marriage is not working well, you need to take the time to ask your spouse about the things you might be doing wrong. And then do not try to talk your spouse out of the answers he or she gave you. God does not heal marriages; people do! So, unless you are willing to make some changes, God cannot heal your marriage. You need God's help, but unless you are willing to change, God will not do anything.

If you really love someone, then you want to encourage that person. If you really love someone, then you want the person to feel appreciated. We need to quit trying to change each other and start giving our partners the love, encouragement, and acceptance they need.

Men And Women Are Different

Men, you need to learn to talk to your woman with words, touch, and a lot of affection. Women need a lot of embraces because they need to feel loved. God made men to be work-oriented, and He made women to be socially-oriented. This is why women need to hear encouraging words to be fulfilled in their lives.

Men and women respond to each other in different ways. When men are stressed out they will try to escape by being alone. Men try to escape through a football game. Women have a hard time understanding this, and they sometimes take it as rejection. Many times when a woman is stressed out she wants to be with people. She loves to get on the phone and talk about the problem. It is her way of working things out.

> *If you are married and your marriage is not working well, you need to take the time to ask your spouse about the things you might be doing wrong.*

The differences between men and women are very simple. When there is a problem, men do not want to talk about it at all. But, when women have a problem, they want to talk about it continually. Men in general are risk takers, but women are usually not. Men will do crazy things to achieve their goals because they are goal-oriented.

Women tend to be more security-minded and not as adventurous. A man can move from house to house or city to city without any problem. But, a woman wants to be settled and to feel the security of her home. Left to themselves, men can go to extremes in many areas of their lives. Men need the wholeness and balance that women bring to life.

Men think they are communicating love by going to work

and bringing home a paycheck, but a woman needs to be told that she is loved. She needs to feel as though she and her husband are best friends. She needs for her man to listen to her because it is part of the way she hears love. Men, if you do not talk to your wife, then someone will come along and talk to her for you. A man becomes attractive when he will listen and when he will share himself with a woman.

TRUST IS AN ISSUE

One major problem area in a marriage has to do with finances. You need to talk about money, and you need to come into agreement about your budgeting. Troubles come when

> *The differences between men and women are very simple. When there is a problem, men do not want to talk about it at all. But, when women have a problem, they want to talk about it continually.*

one spends money without being accountable to the other. You need to reach the point in your relationship where neither of you go off and buy things without talking about it first. Financial harmony requires honesty and mutual respect.

There is no question that men have a difficult time opening up and being intimate about their heart's secrets. So, when a man trusts a woman enough to talk to her, it is important that she keep it to herself and not divulge the information to her friends. If he thinks you are discussing his business with someone else, then he will feel betrayed. If he feels betrayed, then he will distance himself.

If you do not trust your husband or your wife, it is only a matter of time until you destroy each other. A lack of trust makes you very vulnerable to adultery with someone who seems trustworthy. If you do not trust, you will always be suspicious and think the worst about each other.

A woman needs attention and encouraging words from her man because she sees herself as her man sees her. So, when a man is critical of his wife, she does not feel loved. But, when he says, "Oh, baby, you are so fine," she begins to grow under his leadership.

When the man can meet the emotional needs of his wife, he will eventually receive all of the respect he needs. When a man makes his wife feel loved, she will give him all that he needs in abundance. If you are speaking negatively about your spouse, then stop today. God says, married couples are to "become one flesh" (Gen. 2:24). This means that when you make negative remarks about your spouse, you are speaking negatively about yourself.

Why did the children of God stay in the wilderness for forty years? They were delayed from going into the Promised Land because of their murmuring, backbiting, and their negativity. If you will build up your spouse properly, he or she will never be looking for approval from someone else. The only person who can steal your spouse is the one who knows how to encourage your spouse more than you do.

Men, you need to know that your wife will become whatever you call her. When you brag on her, she has a way of becoming what you call her. God intends for the man to protect and to cover the backs of his family. To cover their backs means that he never tells secret or hurtful things about his spouse or his children; he builds them

> *If you do not trust your husband or your wife, it is only a matter of time until you destroy each other.*

up when speaking about them to others. If a wife feels covered, then she will have no problem respecting and admiring her husband.

If your wife does not look better today than when you married her, it could be because she eventually became the negative things you said about her. You can get it turned around today by saying things like, "Baby, you are so fine. I am so lucky to have you in my life." Sometimes you have to "call those things which do not exist as though they did" (Rom. 4:17).

ENCOURAGE EACH OTHER

Whether or not you know it, your wife is an extension of yourself. When my wife leaves the house, I want her to look the best that she can. This is why I do everything possible to put her first in every way in my life.

The right kind of man will encourage his wife, and he will make sacrifices for her. The right kind of wife does not pull against her husband or nag him even when he is wrong. She prays for him and does her part to have his back covered.

3

AFTER THE WEDDING COMES THE MARRIAGE

While men and women have different callings on their lives, when couples come together to form the lifelong relationship we call "marriage," God is not a mere passive observer. He is vitally interested and wants to see a spiritual union between the two partners as they work to nurture and support each other while complying with God's order for the home. That order refers to the complementary roles of husband and wife.

Men and women have different roles in a marriage relationship. The man is to be the spiritual leader. He is to be the protector, the provider, and the warrior of the house. God's definition of a man is very different from the world's.

God says that a man should love his wife as Christ loved the church. Since Christ sacrificed His life for the church, it seems clear that a man is not supposed to be a dictator over his wife (Eph. 5:25). He is to be an example to his family, and he is to be the disciplinarian in the family.

> *A man is supposed to be submissive to God's Word. He is to rule and to reign and to take dominion over all of the works of the devil. He is to lead his family in prayer...*

A man is supposed to be submissive to God's Word. He is to rule and to reign and to take dominion over all of the works of the devil. He is to lead his family in prayer and to wash his wife in the water of the Word (Eph. 5:26).

GOD'S CALLING ON MEN

Men are to be the visionaries for the family. Most men are not concerned with minor problems that may occur in the family. Most men are concerned with the big picture, not with the details. In fact, most men are oblivious to details.

For example, sometimes when I come home, my wife will ask me how the house looks. Knowing that she has just spent a couple of hours cleaning it, I will say, "It looks wonderful." But the truth is that I never even noticed how clean things were when I came in the house. It's not that I don't care, I just don't see the details.

God has called men to be the leaders of the family. We are to be protectors and warriors. We are called to "fight the good fight of faith" (1 Tim. 6:12).

We are called to be hunters and to provide for our families. Most men are weekend warriors as they watch basketball, football, or some other sport. It is a man's way of displaying the warrior spirit. When he goes fishing, or goes shopping, or drives the car, he is displaying the hunter spirit.

Men are hunters by nature. A man will pursue and romance a woman until he wins her. A man will use romance in order to conquer his prey. After the conquest, however, some men will move on to other prey. Other men

> *Men are hunters by nature. A man will pursue and romance a woman until he wins her. A man will use romance in order to conquer his prey.*

will put great effort into winning and marrying their sweethearts, but afterwards turn all their energies and attention to sports, business, or even the ministry.

We need to remember that after the wedding comes the marriage. Marriage is not so much about finding the perfect person as it is meeting the needs of the one whom you married. Marriage is not about feelings; it is about commitment. You made a commitment to the Lord first, then to the person whom you married. Real men honor their commitments.

The problem is that many men have wrong ideas about what real manhood is. Our media-driven culture offers many flawed models of masculinity to young boys, so it's no wonder many grow up confused. This is especially true if there is no strong, responsible male influence in their lives.

> *The Biblical model for masculinity is the servant-leader as portrayed by Jesus Christ. This kind of man wins followers by his love and service to others...*

The Biblical model for masculinity is the servant-leader as portrayed by Jesus Christ. This kind of man wins followers by his love and service to others, especially those in his immediate family.

Unfortunately, many men have never experienced that kind of leadership so their innate drive to be a leader may become distorted into the domination or oppression of others.

Such men may try to lord over women, treat them as second-class citizens, abuse women or be disrespectful towards them.

But if you are a Godly man, you must strive to treat everyone as you would want to be treated. And in regard to your wife, you are to love, honor, and cherish her, and to be subject to one another.

In other words, men must give of themselves constantly in order to truly show love and honor. God tells us to nurture our wives because they are bone of our bone and flesh of our flesh (Gen. 2:23).

Men are supposed to be examples of love for the entire family. But society tries to tell us that if men are sensitive, then they are not masculine. God created us to be kind, loving, and affectionate. Men were created to give hugs and kisses to their wives all the time. Husbands are to love their wives as Christ loved the church (Eph. 5:25).

> *Men are supposed to be examples of love for the entire family. But society tries to tell us that if men are sensitive, then they are not masculine.*

Men have been called to die to self, live for the Lord, and live to meet their wives' needs. We are to put her first and give up our selfish desires. Among other things, this means that we cannot go out and buy a bassboat or a motorcycle before we take care of the needs of our wives.

GOD'S CALLING ON WOMEN

The woman was created to be the help-meet. The husband is the head, but make no mistake about the fact that the woman is the neck that turns the head.

What most men do not realize is that they were created to need help. Every man must come to the point where he realizes he needs the strengths a woman brings to a marriage. He must realize that he needs her tenderness, her organizational skills, and her support.

> *The husband is the head, but make no mistake about the fact that the woman is the neck that turns the head.*

If a husband does not take his place as the spiritual head of his household, then God will anoint the wife to take his place. However, it is never the same as when a man does the job God has called him to do.

You can be the most wonderful mother in the world and still watch your children self-destruct because without the presence of an involved father, children tend to act up and get into trouble. It takes a man to bring proper authority into the home.

Besides, God has not called women with children to be the head of the household, to go to the work place, or provide financially for their families. Anytime women are put into all these roles, their children will grow up very rebellious.

God made man out of the dust of the earth, but woman was pulled out of man. She was made from man himself. A woman is looking for the protection she needs and that is why she is so security conscious.

It is important that she feels the protection and the covering of her husband. She needs to know that he will go to battle for her. She needs to know that he will protect her and that he has her back covered.

Generally speaking, a girl who lives with her parents is under the covering of her father. But, after she marries, then she is under the covering of her husband.

A woman is looking for the protection she needs and that is why she is so security conscious.

If a woman is single or if the father is not a part of a woman's life, then she is under the prayer covering of her pastor. It is a fatherly covering for her protection.

If you are a single woman, then you must not confuse the covering of a pastor with the covering of a husband. They are not the same thing.

As a woman, you need to know that you are called to be the help-meet in the marriage. You are the one who is to take care of the details of running the home. Many times women get upset because their husbands will not help with the details, but that is not his nature.

God has called the wife to be the help-meet, but that does not mean that she is a slave. This does not mean that she is on her own to do all of the chores, the cleaning, and cook all of the meals like some kind of domestic robot.

It doesn't mean that she raises the children either; it does mean that she is the primary care-giver, especially to the younger children. Men are to be vitally involved in the rearing and training of children. Being a help-meet means that she is a helper, just as the Holy Spirit is God's helper here on earth.

> *As a woman, you need to know that you are called to be the help-mete in the marriage. You are the one who is to take care of the details of running the home.*

One of the primary functions of the wife is to assist the head of the family in promoting Godly principles. It is the helper's job to assist in building wealth for the family.

Because God has anointed the man to be the leader of his house, the devil's plan is to destroy the leader. The devil hates the family, and he is doing everything that he can to destroy the family unit. You must be a woman of prayer and continuously cover your husband in prayer.

Many times a woman becomes critical because her husband is not concerned with details. However, if she criticizes her man enough, she will break his spirit. He may eventually believe that he cannot ever please her and trouble will begin.

If a man loses the warrior spirit, then he will lose his vision for his family. In fact, if he loses the warrior spirit, then he probably will not do well on his job or in his business. "Where there is no vision, the people perish" (Prov. 29:18). When a man is fulfilling his destiny, then he is full of dreams and full of visions. When he has the strength and the support of a loving wife, then he is unstoppable.

> *Many times a woman becomes critical because her husband is not concerned with details. However, if she criticizes her man enough, she will break his spirit.*

Women today are frustrated because their men have no vision. God has called the man to be the visionary, but if he has no vision, then there is nothing for the wife to support.

If you are not encouraging and affirming your husband, there is a chance he will never become what he should. He needs you to cheer him on, and he needs your strength and support at all times.

It is important for the wife to create an environment of peace in the home. As long as the home is a war zone, the man will not want to come home.

If there is a lot of unrest at home, then he may try to find peace somewhere else. Men need touching, and they need your gentleness. It is that gentle touch that brings him assurance and rest in his soul.

MARRIAGE TAKES TWO SUPPORTING PEOPLE

A man can build a house, but a woman has the talent and gift of building a home. A man can work all day fighting as a warrior in the work place, but when he comes home, he needs his wife to bring healing to his warrior spirit. When men go off to the work place they perform better if they have the support of their wives.

A woman who criticizes her warrior can cause him to quit. But, when she praises him, then he will rise to the occasion. When she tells him that there is no one like him, he will flex his muscles and fight for her even more.

The Bible talks about wives submitting to their husbands (Eph. 5:22). There are many times in a woman's life that she has to do so by faith. But, anytime a woman or a man chooses to obey God's Word and submit by faith, it is always for the best.

If you will make up your mind to pursue God's plan for your life, then you will eventually have success.

Sometimes you have to walk by faith and not by sight when it comes to your marriage. You need to stop talking about all the things your husband cannot do and tell him what a good man he is.

And, let me say that the same thing is true about your children. Begin to praise them for their good qualities instead of always criticizing them. If you want to see changes take place in your spouse and in your children, then you must learn to give them positive reinforcement. As long as there is unrest and insecurity in their lives, it is hard for them to hear God's voice.

When a woman learns to encourage her man, she will instill a fighting spirit within him. If she brings peace into his life, then she will be the neck that turns the head.

A woman can add to a man's confidence or she can steal his self esteem. She can create an environment of rest or she can criticize him to the point that he will never want to come home.

A man needs to be admired and respected. Your man needs affirmation so badly that if you do not give it to him, he may find someone else who will. Anytime a woman is in strong competition with her husband, there is going to be trouble.

> *If you want to see changes take place in your spouse and in your children, then you must learn to give them positive reinforcement.*

If your husband feels that you are competing with him, it will make him feel as though you do not respect him and his place of authority.

Because men have abused their power in the past, there is a spirit among women today that is referred to as a Jezebel spirit. It is a man-hating spirit that will not submit to men and has no respect for men. Be careful that you do not take on this spirit and that you do not try to control your husband.

It is not your responsibility to make him do anything. It is your responsibility to give advice, if he wants it, and then to pray. The more you try to make him do something, such as go to church, the more he will rebel. The more you try to make him do anything, the more disrespect he will feel.

> *Your man needs affirmation so badly that if you do not give it to him, he may find someone else who will.*

If he is so bullheaded that he will not listen to you, then God is able to use failure to bring correction to him. Remember, the just shall "walk by faith, not by sight" (2 Cor. 5:7).

The man is to be the king of his castle and the woman is to be his queen. Every woman must treat her husband with respect or there will be trouble. There cannot be peace in the home if two people are trying to lead. There must be leadership and there must be submission.

However, there cannot be submission unless you submit. If a woman does not submit to her husband properly, she will not see her prayers answered, and if a husband doesn't honor his wife, he will not see his prayers answered either.

Peter calls the woman a weaker vessel (1 Peter 3:7), but this does not mean she is a second-class citizen nor does this mean that she is inferior. This does not give a man the right to put her down.

When a wife honors her husband, even at times when he doesn't deserve it, she is honoring God. When your husband feels your faith and your confidence in him, then he is more likely to obey God.

A lot of women will not submit to their husbands until their husbands get right with God. What they do not realize is that when they submit to their husbands, their husbands are more easily turned to God.

When a husband sees the love of Jesus Christ in you, then he is more likely to make a move toward serving God. This is why some women need to spend more time ministering to their husbands and less time on the phone.

You must learn to build up your spouse and never belittle him or her in front of others. Every time you see something good about your spouse, praise them. Learn to build up your mate publicly.

If you are going to have a happy marriage, then you need to love your spouse as he or she is, because if you set out to change your mate, there is likely to be trouble.

You need to talk about each other's strengths, not the weaknesses. James said that the tongue is like a rudder, and it will guide your entire life (James 3:4-5). If God can get you to control your words, then He can guide you and He can control your entire life.

> ...some women need to spend more time ministering to their husbands and less time on the phone.

Words are like seeds that reproduce after their own kind. Words either kill or they build a relationship. They either encourage or they discourage the ones to whom you talk.

Jesus said it is not what enters a man that defiles him, but what comes out of his mouth (Matt. 15:11). Your future can be predicted by what you are saying today. "Death and life are in the power of the tongue, and those who love it will eat its fruit" (Prov. 18:21).

This is why God tells us to speak things by faith. This is why He tells us to prophesy to the dry bones (Ezek. 37:4). Sometimes you have to speak life to a dead marriage.

God calls husbands and wives to be one flesh. No one is superior in a marriage, but God defines our roles. Every husband needs a wife he can trust. Every wife needs a husband who will provide for her, protect her, and listen to her. Every wife needs to know that her husband values her and that he will encourage her to be all that she can be.

Every husband needs a wife who will listen to him without

trying to change him and without trying to criticize him. Every husband needs the support and the strength of a loving wife. Every wife needs a husband who will love her as Christ loved the church. Every wife needs to know that even when she makes a mistake, she is loved and that her husband has her back covered.

It is time to encourage one another. It is time to repent and confess to each other that you have not been as good a husband or as good a wife as you should have been.

> *Every husband needs a wife he can trust. Every wife needs a husband who will provide for her, protect her, and listen to her.*

It is time to change your actions and to change your words. It is time to build each other up and dream about your future together. It is time to build a lasting relationship and love each other the way you need to be loved. After the wedding comes the marriage. With God's help and His guidance, the two of you can make it work.

4

LOVE ME THE WAY
THAT I NEED TO BE LOVED

Lasting relationships and strong marriages are built on our love for each other and our love for God. Without God's love and His Word in our lives, we cannot love the way we should. If we cannot love each other the way we should, then we cannot put our houses in order. Only God can help us do this, and only God can give us the ability to love each other.

There is something that we need in our lives in order for us to be happy and well adjusted. It is to be loved and to give love to others. People will do almost anything to be loved. They will make compromises, they will sleep around, and they will even be unfaithful in a marriage. The truth is that we will make fools of ourselves and spend every dime we have just to be loved.

Love is so powerful that it will heal you when no doctor can. When you have love in your life, you have a strength that will get you through almost anything. People who do not experience real love will tend to quit.

The root of every emotional problem we have is a lack of love. If there is fear in your life, if you have problems with rejection, or if you have mental problems, it is probably because of a lack of love.

> *Love is so powerful that it will heal you when no doctor can. When you have love in your life, you have a strength that will get you through almost anything.*

People will risk everything they have in order to be loved the way they need to be. When marriages are in trouble, it is because someone's needs are not being met.

Our need to be loved is so great that it can outweigh common sense. If you look at good marriages, you will find two people who are determined to meet each other's needs. When you find a bad marriage, it is because one or both parties are not meeting their partner's love need.

If you want to have a great marriage, sit down with your spouse, and find out what he or she wants you to do. You need to find out the way your mate hears or feels love. Just because you need love one way does not mean your partner needs it in the same way.

People hear love or feel love differently. If you can understand the way people feel love, and you work hard at nurturing this, then you will have a tremendous life. People tend to love their spouses the way they themselves feel love. We need to go beyond this and start reaching out to our mates with the kind of love they need. When you do this, you will take your marriage to a whole new level.

A COMMAND TO LOVE EACH OTHER

Jesus said, "A new commandment I give to you, that you love one another; as I have loved you, that you also love one another" (John 13:34). It is not an option; it is a command.

> *People tend to love their spouses the way they themselves feel love. We need to go beyond this and start reaching out to our mates with the kind of love they need.*

Christian marriages are ending in divorce in record numbers. Why? The awful truth is that many people simply do not know how to love each other. Many of us were raised by parents who did not know how to love, and whose parents did not know how to love either. We pass this on from generation to generation.

We need Jesus in our lives so that we can learn how to love each other the way we should. Jesus said, "If you love me, you will keep My commandments" (John 14:15). Thus, if you do not keep His commandments, then you do not love Him.

Sometimes you hear people say, "You have to love me unconditionally in our marriage," or, "This is the way I am, and you must accept me this way." Do you believe you have to love each other unconditionally in marriage? God's love for us is unconditional. A parent's love for a child should be unconditional.

> *We need to take responsibility and grow up if things are going to get better. It's all about giving and working together...*

And, there are certain ways we must treat each other in a marriage, if we are going to be successful. However, we cannot use this "unconditional love" line as a way to get away from changing what each of us know we need to change.

We need to take responsibility and grow up if things are going to get better. It's all about giving and working together to better the relationship. If you do not receive what you need in a marriage, then you will either build walls around yourself or you will leave the relationship. You will either shut down emotionally or you will get a divorce.

Some honest examination needs to go on between couples in order to determine if the problems are really being worked on or if you are hiding behind things to look good and avoid dealing with the issues that are killing the marriage.

Occasionally you'll meet Christian couples, and as you see them around from time to time, everything seems great, and their marriage seems fine. Then one day you'll be shocked to hear that they are divorced, and soon afterwards you may hear they are remarried to someone else.

> *...honest examination needs to go on between couples in order to determine if the problems are really being worked on or if you are hiding...*

This happens because some Christians come to church with masks on, and they refuse to share with anyone about their problems because they are afraid people will judge them.

But until you have lived with someone or until you have walked in someone's shoes, you have no idea what they have been through, and you have no right to judge other people.

If you are in a Christian marriage today, and your mate does not know how to love you, you can feel cheated in your life. If left undealt with, this will lead you and your spouse to becoming roommates instead of help-meets, and make you susceptible to an adulterous relationship. You must do something to save your marriage.

Christian people do not divorce those who love them the way they need to be loved. Christians are not usually looking around or being unfaithful to their spouses unless they are hurting and not being loved properly. So, what do you fight about all the time?

What issues keep coming up in your relationship that are always a point of contention? If you will examine those things, you will probably find a lack of love is the root of these issues. If you will make it your goal to learn to love your mate the way he or she needs to be loved, your entire life will change.

> *What issues keep coming up in your relationship that are always a point of contention?*

Because people hear or feel love in different ways, they have different needs. Meeting those needs may require a little creativity.

No one can know for certain if another will love flowers or phone calls during the day or other special expressions without talking about what makes each partner feel love. The point is, when someone we love does not meet our needs, we shouldn't get mad, rather we should be willing to sit down, lay aside our pride, be honest, and tell each other the way we hear and feel love.

Other people's needs may seem ridiculous to us, but that is because we are all different. Men and women's needs are far from the same. I've heard women say time and again, "If he really loved me, he would know what I needed." You need to understand that men are not mind readers. You have to tell your spouse what you want and precisely what you need.

Occasionally I hear, "Well, Pastor, if it's not in his heart, I don't want him to even try." If you really mean this, then self-pity has taken over and you need to work on your attitude so he will not get frustrated and give up. Remember, you have to tell your mate exactly what you want and what you need.

> *You need to understand that men are not mind readers. You have to tell your spouse what you want and precisely what you need.*

You must be willing to communicate and to give time for actions and heart attitudes to change in both of you.

Before you got married, you always tried to meet the other person's needs. It seems as though people change after they get married. They become comfortable in the relationship, and they stop trying.

You can feel cheated because your partner has changed. This is why it is so important to go to premarital counseling. It is very important that you establish whether or not you can meet the other person's needs. If you cannot meet their needs, then it is time to move on.

Love Needs Communication and Understanding

Each of us has needs in our lives that are nonnegotiable. We have wants and desires, but there are some core matters that must be met. What are yours? In general, men have a greater sexual need than do women.

For most men sex would be at the top of their list. On the other hand, most women have a need to be first in their man's life.

But, you have to tell each other what being first means in practical terms. Does that mean that you want your husband to open the door for you and pull out your chair to be seated? Or does it mean that you want him to send the kids to relatives and sweep you off for a romantic getaway?

Maybe your husband treats you like one of the boys when the way you feel love is being treated like a lady. Maybe your wife belittles you, so you do not feel loved or respected. Whatever the reason, you need to sit down and tell each other what it takes to make you feel loved and important.

Whether or not you know it, men have a great need to be admired and respected. Men need the approval of their wives in almost everything they do. Please do not sit down and try to discuss these issues when you are angry because nothing will get accomplished when a spirit of anger dominates the conversation.

Most people have a need to have an attractive spouse. We want someone of whom we can be proud. If you no longer care about the way you look, then you could have some problems in your marriage. You need to find out what your spouse likes in hair, clothes, weight, makeup, etc., and then try to meet their needs.

> *...you need to sit down and tell each other what it takes to make you feel loved and important.*

Sometimes our spouse's needs are the same as ours. When this takes place, it is very easy to meet those needs. But, this does not happen very often so we must assume that each of us should work on carefully listening. How does your spouse hear love?

If you yell at them, they may think of you as a parent. They need a spouse, not a dad or mom. If you would stop yelling, you just might discover your spouse to be a completely different person.

One way you may hear love is to do things together. If you want to go camping, then ask your mate to go with you. If your partner wants to go to the baseball game, go with your mate and gradually learn how the game is played. It does not matter whether or not you like the activity; if your spouse does, then you need to join him or her in it.

The truth is that if people do not have a support system of

love around them, they probably won't make it. They will risk losing everything to find loving support when all you need to do is provide it for them.

> *The truth is that if people do not have a support system of love around them, they probably won't make it. They will risk losing everything to find loving support...*

But if you are making all of the major decisions in your family without consulting your spouse, you may be communicating that you do not think your mate is important enough to consult. This may cause your spouse to feel unloved.

People can always find good reasons for shutting down a relationship. So the real question is, are you willing to make whatever changes are necessary to correct the situation? If not, then it cannot be fixed.

Your spiritual enemy's strategy is to stop the flow of love in your life. If he can hurt you, then he is happy. If he can break up your marriage, then he's accomplishing his goal.

If he can isolate you through depression, then he is happy. But you are to stand against him by taking action and protecting what is yours. You are not to let him win by default, that is, by your inaction; so get to work on your marriage, and give no place to the devil (Eph. 4:27).

LOVE IS AN ATTITUDE

What is love? The world says love is butterflies, warm fuzzies, and a knot in your stomach. But, it is more than that. Love is the way we treat each other. It is a decision about the way we meet other people's needs. It is more than saying, "I love you." It is more than a hug or a kiss.

It is making a decision to be careful about what we say to each other, and how we treat one another. Love is an attitude. Love is watching our tongues and the words we say to each other. Love does not criticize; it encourages. Love is kind; it is not jealous (1 Cor. 13:4).

> *Your spiritual enemy's strategy is to stop the flow of love in your life. If he can hurt you, then he is happy.*

Paul tells us that love is meeting the needs of others. He said that you can have all the money in the world, but if you do not know how to love, then you have nothing. He said that it does not matter how spiritual you are, if you do not know how to love people, then you are nothing, and you have nothing. He said that you can sell everything you have and give it to the poor, but if you do not know how to love people, then it is of no value (1 Cor. 13:3).

Legalistic people live by the letter of the law and they show no mercy. They are generally mean, show very little love, and don't seem to understand how to be kind. Paul said that love is kind (1 Cor. 13:4).

But some church folks are the meanest people on the face of the earth. This is usually a result of not liking themselves. Mean people do not know how to love. Some people will never receive the love they need from their families.

This is why it is so important that when they walk into a church, they receive love and understanding, and realize that they will not be judged. The gospel is all about love and forgiveness. Jesus and God are all about love. The church should be all about love too.

Love does not say, "I love you" in church and then tear someone apart with words when they get home. Anytime there is a lack of love between two people, demonic activity is increased. Anytime the flow of love is stopped, the devil will win.

Paul said you can call yourself a prophet, but if you do not know how to love people, then you have nothing (1 Cor. 13:2). You can live in a mansion, but if you do not know how to walk in love, then you have nothing. You can have butlers and maids waiting on you hand and foot, but if you do not know how to love, your life will be empty.

You can prophesy with the best of them, but if you do not know how to help people with the spirit of gentleness, then you are nothing (Gal. 6:1).

So the question is this: Are you loving your companion the way he or she needs to be loved, and are you willing to meet his or her needs?

Your relationship may not be able to be saved unless you can answer this question positively and mean it. The first step is to get God's love into our hearts. But we cannot stop here.

We must take the love God places inside of us and use it to reach our families. It will take courage, and it will take time. But every step we take to heal and love will be matched with a power from the Holy Spirit to continually move forward. Yes, God will help, but He wants us to put in the effort needed to turn things around. As we strive to do everything possible, God will handle the impossible!

5

CONSTRUCTING A HEALTHY FAMILY

As we all know, the family unit is under great stress today. It's God's plan that family members learn to love God with all of their hearts and learn to love their neighbors as themselves. The purpose of the family unit is to bring honor to God in some way.

God shows the relationship that Christ has with the church so He could teach us how we are to relate to one another in relationships. God has plainly set forth in His Word that every husband and father is to wash his household with the water of the Word daily.

God intends for the male to be the spiritual head of his family and the wife is to be the supporter or the helper. God said that He was looking for a man to build up a hedge, or wall of righteousness, so that judgment would not fall on the land. I'll say it another way as well: God is looking for the man to pray in his house so that judgment doesn't fall on his house.

God intends for every man to be the spiritual head of his family and lead the members of his family in righteousness, in prayer, and by example. He is to love his wife and live with His wife in an understanding way.

> *God intends for every man to be the spiritual head of his family and lead the members of his family in righteousness, in prayer, and by example.*

In other words, he is supposed to know his wife. He is supposed to study his wife. He's supposed to know how she thinks. He is to know what she wants so he knows how to treat her. And then she is to yield to his leadership.

God's Word tells us about order in our homes. There is an order in the Kingdom of God where everything must fit in its place. When everything fits in its place, then there is order.

But anytime someone is not in the proper place, the result will be disorder, disharmony, strife, and, note this — division. That's always your spiritual enemy's plan; divide then conquer.

Don't get the idea that the principle is about position, power, prestige, or right and wrong. It's not. It's not about who's right and wrong, or any of those things. It's about the proper order that God has set forth. But I can tell you that if you will follow God's order in the home and in your life, you will be under His protection.

When you are outside of His order, you are outside of His protection. God uses the family to teach us about authority. God says that husbands are to be yielded unto God, and wives are to be yielded to the husbands.

Anytime the husband is not yielded to God, you are going to have disorder in the home and you're going to have trouble. Anytime the wife is not yielded to her husband, there's going to be a lack of order, and there's going to be trouble in your home. Now please bear with me and read my whole discussion before you get mad at me.

> *When you are outside of His order, you are outside of His protection. God uses the family to teach us about authority.*

God gives us order for the home. This is not my idea; it's God's idea. He says that if you are married, there is an order that you have to follow. If you are a man, you are to be submitted to God's Word. If you are a woman, you are to be submitted to the Lord, yes. But you are also to be submitted to your husband. God didn't say that women were to be submitted to all men or to men in general. God said that a "wife" is to be submitted to her "husband." This is a very important distinction.

Now listen to this, the Bible says that God created man to bring glory to himself. Then God created woman to bring glory to the man.

> When somebody sees your wife, they should see you. And it's all about order. It's about the man bringing glory to God...

If you will understand what God is trying to say, the man is to bring honor and glory to God and the wife is to be so submitted to her husband that when somebody sees her, they see him. When somebody sees your wife, they should see you. And it's all about order. It's about the man bringing glory to God and the woman bringing glory to her man, and through that glory, bringing increased glory to God.

Ladies, if you are single and you cannot submit to the man you are dating, you better get rid of him now. Because the Word says "you are to honor him, you are to admire him and you are to respect him." And if you can't do it now, you're certainly not going to do it after you get married.

Submission is all about walking by faith. Submission doesn't make you a doormat. Submission is about faith. God said it, so therefore, by faith I am going to get in my place. I'm going to get in my order. It's all about faith.

No matter who we are we must understand authority, and we must understand yielding to authority. We live in a very rebellious time in history. People don't want to be told what to do or how to live their lives.

Let me tell you, the children of Israel wandered in the wilderness because they questioned the authority over them. They were in the wilderness 40 years because they were murmuring and grumbling against their God-appointed authority. They wandered in the wilderness and never went into the Promised Land because of their doubt and unbelief concerning what God had told them about order and authority.

Even Christians say, "Don't tell me I have to go to church to be a Christian. Don't tell me I have to tithe. Don't tell where to park my car. Don't tell me what seat I have to sit in. Don't tell me that I have to submit to authority because I hear God too."

> *Submission doesn't make you a doormat. Submission is about faith.*

Isn't that exactly what Miriam did to Moses? "Don't tell me I have to submit to Moses' authority. I hear God too" (paraphrased). And God said, "Okay, Miriam, you want to backbite the man of God, we'll just let some leprosy come on you and see if we can get your attention" (paraphrased).

The point I'm trying to make is this; there is protection when you come under authority. You see, it's very simple. It's either submission or rebellion. There's nothing in between.

Understand that it's always a challenge because the flesh is fighting us every inch of the way. The challenge is the flesh against the Spirit. The things of the flesh against the things of God. That's always the challenge, and as Christians, we'll face that challenge until the day we die.

> *God requires that every human being be under authority. Whether it is your pastor or your neighbor, or somebody in the choir.*

God requires that every human being be under authority. Whether it is your pastor or your neighbor, or somebody in the choir. Whether it is the wife submitted to her husband, a child to his parents, or a businessman to his boss. Every human being has to be under authority otherwise they'll become a renegade doing their own thing.

God's law says that if you can't submit to human authority then you will never be able to submit to heavenly authority. Submission is slavery unless you are living by faith. Unless you have the Word of God in your heart, submission is restrictive and confining. But when you've got the Word of God in your heart and are living by faith, submission brings peace. Your attitude becomes, "Yes, Lord, show me what to do."

It takes faith to live this way. It takes faith to believe that God is correcting your spouse when they're wrong. It takes faith to believe that God is working on your boss when you know they're wrong.

God doesn't play favorites. He is not a respecter of social classes or castes or any other man-made social division. But every football team has to have a quarterback. Every team has to have a leader. Somebody has to lead, and somebody has to bring support. Somebody has to throw the ball and somebody has to block for the man throwing the ball. That's true in sports, in human institutions, and it's true in marriage.

> *...when you've got the Word of God in your heart and are living by faith, submission brings peace.*

Anytime we defy authority we are saying we don't trust God. God has called the man to lead the team, and the wife is to be the helper of the team. But if you think that being the helper makes you a second-rate citizen, remember that the Holy Spirit is God's helper on this earth. They are a team; and in fact, the Trinity models in several ways the unity, diversity, and submission found in the marriage relationship.

Remember, God has called you and your mate to be a team. Your wife cannot follow unless you lead. Your husband cannot lead your family unless you follow him.

Ladies, there's something inside every woman that wants to

take control, but unless you cooperate and allow your husband to lead, he'll never succeed in the way God desires.

Here's the big challenge for a submissive wife. Suppose he is leading, and you tell him which direction to go, but he doesn't do what you told him to do. He made a big mistake and now you want to tell him, "I told you so."

It happens. Our recurring task in submission to authority is to be patient when you know the one in authority is going the wrong way, doing the wrong things. The temptation is to say: "I told you what to do, and you didn't listen, and now look at the mess you got us in to." The greatest challenge is for you to keep your peace, sit back and pray.

> *...there's something inside every woman that wants to take control, but unless you cooperate and allow your husband to lead, he'll never succeed in the way God desires.*

Ladies, please listen to me. You are so important to your husband's success that if you don't encourage him, he may not make it. Now he's not going to tell you that, but there's a little boy inside him that has to be encouraged, that has to be loved, that has to be told he's wonderful when you know he's not there yet.

Let me tell you, if you are a single woman, you need to learn to be an encourager right now. If you're in a dating relationship, learn to be a team player. Learn to be supportive.

Learn to be an encourager with whatever he's doing. Practice being under authority now. Your words will either encourage him or discourage him. Your words will either give him strength or your words will slow him down. If you are going to construct a healthy family in this new millennium, he has to feel your strength and your support. Remember, submission to authority means I am walking by faith and not by feelings.

> *You are so important to your husband's success that if you don't encourage him, he may not make it.*

The Word says, "that women are to bring honor to their husband." She is to show honor, admiration, and respect. She needs to build him up and encourage him. A man will fall deeply in love with a woman that tells him he's wonderful, that encourages him, and that respects him.

Because men need honor and respect, a woman must be very careful of the way she talks to her man. Think of it this way; do you bring your husband honor? Examine that. A team becomes undefeatable when everybody is in agreement. When one team member is pulling away, it will always cause an undercurrent of tension. It causes trouble, it causes strife, it causes division.

The Bible says that one can put a thousand to flight but two can put ten thousand to flight. What does that mean? It means if you're in agreement, you've got power. When there's division, you have dissipated your power.

Your spiritual enemy knows that when the two of you get serious and come into agreement over your children, he knows it's not going to be long before you're going to kick the devil out. The enemy also knows that when the two of you get serious and come into agreement over your finances, it won't be long until all of your bills are going to be paid. And the enemy knows that when the two of you become deadly earnest and get into agreement, it won't be long and you're going to get that house you want.

> *A team becomes undefeatable when everybody is in agreement. When one team member is pulling away, it will always cause an undercurrent of tension.*

Remember, God has an order, and as long as you are in that order, everything is going to work out. Submission always defeats the enemy's plans. Ladies, if you marry a man that is not submitted to the Lord, you are going to have a very difficult life.

Here's the other side of it. If you married a man knowing that he wasn't sold out and submitted to the Lord, you're going to be in trouble. Everyone tried to tell you not to marry him, but you did it anyway. You wouldn't listen. And now you don't know what to do with him. You made your decision so now you need to stay and try to work things out and believe God. That's hard, but don't misunderstand that statement. God doesn't expect you to put up with abuse.

But God's Word says not to be unequally yoked. Here's the bottom line. Submit to the authority of God's Word. That's all you have to do. Do what God says and don't question it. Let me tell you. You must not date unbelievers because you will get tricked. And you'll think that just because you met them in church that they're living for God.

If your children are rebellious, the first thing I would check is the order in your home. If your children are rebellious, is the man submitted to God? Is the wife submitted to her husband? Is there order in the home.

If God can teach us to submit to earthly authority, then He can teach us to be in submission to His Word. If He can teach you to be submitted to unreasonable people, then when He tells you "don't do something" and you want to do it, you'll say, "Okay, Lord."

> *God has an order, and as long as you are in that order, everything is going to work out. Submission always defeats the devil's plans.*

That's the whole point in submission. Submission isn't submission until you don't want to do it and you do it anyway, with a good attitude. And the point is if He can teach you to submit to unreasonable people, then He knows He can speak to you, and you'll do whatever He tells you to do.

Remember that God wants all of us to be under authority so He can teach us about obedience. We have to submit to our employers. If we don't submit to our employers, we usually get fired. We are to submit to church leaders. Most men didn't have a clue about submission until they got saved and came into church. Now they are in the process of learning about submission.

> *If your children are rebellious, the first thing I would check is the order in your home.*

Let me tell you one reason to be under the authority of your pastor and your church leader. The Word says that they are responsible for your soul. God deals with His leaders in a much stricter way than He does anybody else. When I tell you to be under authority, it's only for your protection and training. A man that cannot love an unreasonable wife is probably a man that cannot submit to the Word of God because God told us to love our wives even when they aren't reasonable.

A wife that cannot submit to her husband, is a wife that probably cannot submit to all of God's Word. Submission is about humility. You have to be humble to submit because pride says I don't have to submit to anybody.

The Bible says that God has a purpose in marriage. The

purpose is to glorify Him, and to build a healthy family through teamwork. May I say that being the spiritual leader of a wife can be a difficult task? This is because the leader has some tremendous responsibilities in the leading of his wife.

The devil has done everything he can to attack the leadership of men in the home. He tempts men with things that are unbelievable: drugs, pornography, adultery, because he knows if he can cut off the head, the rest of the body is going to be die.

The enemy has attacked our young men so that he can steal their masculinity, steal their leadership and steal their headship. Psychologists today say that children obtain their sexual identity from their father. If a father is absent, then children may grow up very confused about their sexuality.

Unless a little girl has the love of a father, she may go anywhere, even to the streets, to find the love of a man. Without a father's leadership, a boy is capable of almost anything. There's something about a father's love that brings stability to a child.

Let me tell you, Eve listened to the serpent instead of listening to her husband. If she had been listening to her husband, she would never have gotten into that mess. Ladies, be careful of the voices you are listening to. The word *husband* means "house band." It's the husband that's supposed to band the house together. It's the husband, not the wife, who's supposed to stand up for righteousness and say "as for me and my house we will serve the Lord."

Any male can make a baby. It takes a real man to be a
father. Any male can get a woman pregnant, but it takes a real

> *The devil has done
> everything he can to
> attack the
> leadership of men in
> the home.*

man to say "God, you are first in my
life, and I'm going to have sex with only
one person and that person is my wife."

Now the test comes when you love
God and you're not getting from her
what you need or she is not giving you

what you need. This is the test. Am I submitted to the Word of
God, or do I follow my flesh? If you were to ask the average
Christian woman today what she wants in a man, I believe she
would say "for the man to take his rightful place. For the man
to be loving and nurturing and giving. For the man to accept
responsibility. For the man to be a good provider. For the man
to be humble and say 'I'm sorry' when he makes a mistake. For
the man to ask for help. For the man to protect his family."
And all the women said, "Amen!"

Men, listen to me, your wives and your children are a
product of your leadership. If you were to ask the average
Christian man what he wants in a woman, I believe he would
say "For the woman to be supportive, to honor me, and to be an
encourager."

And I would add, for the woman not to talk down to him,

to respect him, to be a praying woman, and to cover his back at all times. All the men said "Amen!"

Young ladies listen, if you are not a challenge, a man will love you and then leave you. If you are easy for him, in his mind he's saying, "If she's easy for me, she'll be easy for somebody else." If you're not a challenge, you'll always attract the wrong kind of man. If you are a young lady living at home, make that young man come to the house and meet your parents. Don't let him honk the horn and expect you to come running out to him. You have to respect yourself.

> *If you were to ask the average Christian woman today what she wants in a man, I believe she would say "for the man to take his rightful place.*

The reason your man is laying up at home right now is because you made it too easy on him. God made the man to work. A man cannot be fulfilled unless he works. God put the man in the garden and told him to work it.

Ladies, if you have your eye on a man that doesn't work, then he is not your man. You want someone with purpose and vision. He should be a man that's going somewhere with his life and has a job. If he's not willing to work and work hard, he'll never be a provider and he'll never be happy. If you marry such a man, you'll never be happy either. Avoid such men and pray that they grow up.

If you are going to construct a healthy family, you must get your finances in order. Whether you are a man or a woman, you must be responsible in the financial department. You need to set budgets. You have to make a plan. You have to payoff debt so God can help you get that new house.

Men, God called you to be the visionary. That means if you're in debt, you have to give your wife a vision and a plan for how you're going to get out of debt. Stop leaving it up to her to get you out of trouble. You've got to give your wife a plan. Troubles come into a relationship when one person spends money, and they are not accountable to the other person. You'll never build a healthy family until you've got your finances in order.

Ladies, it's in the dating process that you learn what kind of man he really is. It's in the dating process that you find out whether he's going to pay his tithes or not.

You don't need somebody to love you and leave you. You need a Godly man or Godly woman. The Bible says, "he who finds a wife finds a good thing." It's the man that's supposed to be looking for a wife. Ladies, you get into trouble when you're doing the looking and the asking and the paying.

Let me suggest to you ladies, God's posture for you. Put God first. Make Jesus your man. Get involved in your church. Sell out to God. Get so busy working for God that you don't have time for all the disasters your friends are going through all around you.

Then as you're busy with the work of the Lord, God will bring him to you. If you will hear that word, God will save you a lot of trouble, a lot of misery, a lot of grief and shame. It's God's plan that you make Jesus your man and then let Him bring you what you need.

God said that it's not good for man or woman to be alone. God didn't say it wasn't good to be single, He said it's not good to be alone. If you're lonely, it's because you're by yourself. You don't have anybody around you. It's because you eat

> *Men, God called you to be the visionary. That means if you're in debt, you have to give your wife a vision and a plan for how you're going to get out of debt.*

by yourself, ride in the car by yourself, go to the movies by yourself and go out to dinner by yourself. You need to get involved in activities that involve other people.

We're supposed to become one flesh; we're not supposed to have separate bank accounts, we're not supposed to go on separate vacations, we're not supposed to have girls' night out, boys' night out, we are supposed to have two lives blended into one life. The two become one flesh.

Many times the problem is you still haven't given up the independence you had when you were single. You were supposed to give that up when you made your wedding vows. I don't mean that God didn't call us to be individuals. Yes, we are supposed to be individuals. But we are supposed to be married and one flesh.

Men, God's Word wants you to become such a servant to your wife, that she cannot resist your love. I serve my wife beautifully. She never asks me for anything, yet I give her everything I can give her. I'm always looking for some place to take her. My wife gives me all of herself. You see, if you give, it shall be given. The truth of the matter is that when you love your wife, you are loving yourself because the more you do for her, the more you end up doing for yourself.

God said that it's not good for man or woman to be alone. God didn't say it wasn't good to be single.

Ladies, it's important in the dating process that you date a man that will nourish you and cherish you. If he does not nourish you and cherish you single, he's never going to do it after you get married. You want somebody that will bring the best out of you. I saw something in my wife that no other man ever saw, and I'm so glad.

6

BUILDING LASTING
RELATIONSHIPS

The Apostle Paul told Timothy that in the last days difficult times would come. He said mankind would become more and more selfish with the passage of time (2 Tim. 3:1-2). We now live in a society where people are more concerned with their own interests than with meeting the needs of others.

This self-centeredness has permeated every aspect of our lives, including marriage. Paul said that a man "shall leave his father and mother and be joined to his wife" (Eph. 5:31).

For two people to become one flesh requires a moving away from the norms of society and refusing to be self-centered. Marriage, by its very design, requires unselfishness. Marriage, by its very design, will also show you all of the weaknesses you didn't even know you had.

One of the major difficulties in creating great lasting relationships is that men and women are totally different. They think differently and respond differently. Men need physical pleasure, while women need emotional support.

> Relationships require people to be giving and unselfish. Our first inclination is to think about how much we can get from a relationship instead of what we can give.

The Bible says that when you are married, your body does not belong just to you. It belongs to your spouse (1 Cor. 7:4).

When you deny your husband access to physical pleasure, then you open the door for the enemy to come into your life.

When you deny your wife emotional support, then you open the door for the enemy to come into your life again.

Relationships require people to be giving and unselfish. Our first inclination is to think about how much we can get from a relationship instead of what we can give.

Put God First In Relationships

In the old covenant, the man was the central figure of the

home. In the new covenant, Jesus becomes the central figure. So the Lord is to be the head of everything, and we are to be subject to one another.

However, God said that the husband is to spiritually lead his family. A husband is to provide for his family and supply a place to live. The wife is supposed to make the house a comfortable place and give her family a home. She is to create an environment of love and support.

This world is tough, and we all need a place we can retreat to and find some peace. Home should be a place where you feel safe, a place where you are able to hide from the troubles of the world. It is supposed to be a place where your burdens are relieved, not increased. If there is fighting in your house, you need to make up your mind that it is going to stop.

> *Home should be a place where you feel safe, a place where you are able to hide from the troubles of the world.*

Everyone in the family needs to sit down together, agree on a plan, and make a decision that each will do his or her part to make the house a safe place. You need to make a decision that your home is a "no war" zone. Anytime a man goes to the grocery store to get a carton of milk and never returns, it is usually because his house was not a place of refuge.

It is difficult to go into the world and fight everyday, and then come home to more fighting. And because of the special load single parents have to carry, they have a desperate need for a place of refuge and safety.

> *Where there is a constant struggle for peace, it is only a matter of time until something gives.*

But we all need a place of love, understanding, and support for the burdens we are carrying. Where there is a constant struggle for peace, it is only a matter of time until something gives.

The pressures of this world are greater than ever, and the demands within our families are escalating. Because of these forces, the need for loving homes that are a haven from the stresses of modern life is absolutely crucial. The last thing we need is conflict within the home, and the only way to create lasting relationships of love is for husbands and wives to make strong commitments to the Lord.

It needs to dawn on us that God's way is always the best way, and we need to diligently seek Him to help us handle the pressures we battle daily.

PRAYER BRINGS PEACE TO RELATIONSHIPS

Getting into a battle with a family member shows that there is something wrong in your relationship with the Lord. When you respond in love to a harsh situation, you reveal that your relationship with the Lord is strong. But most of us have not made this "walking in love" principle an automatic response. Generally, when someone hurts us, we flare up and want to strike back and/or get even.

We need to make up our minds that even though we are going to be tested, our houses are going to be places of prayer. If prayer is not going on in your family, then your relationship will eventually have trouble. Prayer is the only thing that will keep peace.

Jesus said the greatest commandment was to love the Lord your God with all your heart (Mark 12:30). Then He said that you are to love your neighbor as yourself (Mark 12:31). When you have the love of God in your heart, it is easier to bring peace into your home.

You must choose to forgive, repeatedly. When you think back on the words of Jesus and the example He gave us, then you will recognize the validity of what I'm saying. The truth is, we are to love one another as Christ loved the church.

MARRIAGE IS A COVENANT RELATIONSHIP

What does the marriage covenant mean? It means you will unconditionally love each other no matter what happens. It means you can disagree without hating each other. The marriage covenant means that your strengths are now mine, your friends are now my friends, and your family is now my family.

When two people are in covenant together, "it is all for one and one for all." They are saying, "Together, we can accomplish anything." They are saying, "Nothing can come between us because of our commitment to one another."

"Covenant" means that I will go to the ends of the earth for you. I will do everything in my power to support you and be there for you. I will be there to help bear your burdens. A covenant is a decision, not a feeling. When you make a covenant with someone, you are saying, "I will be there for you in sickness and in health."

A covenant means that we can disagree, but still support one another. The enemy's plan is to cause people to be at odds with one another. His plan is to divide and conquer. He wants to distort the marriage covenant in some way and make people feel isolated.

If we create the impression that we are unhappy with our spouses, then we will generate a lot of insecurity. When we make our mates feel as though they never do enough for us, eventually they will lose heart and walk out of the relationship.

If we make our spouses feel as though they never make enough money, then it is only a matter of time until trouble begins. The issue is, are we really supporting our partners the way they need to be supported?

For example, even if you do not particularly enjoy fishing or the opera, do you go along occasionally to show your support? Similarly, do you encourage your close friends the way God would want? If your friends feel as though you are not satisfied with them, there will be insecurity in those relationships. If you are not encouraging your friends properly, it is only a matter of time until some of them will lose interest in the relationship and drift away from you.

> *A covenant means that we can disagree, but still support one another.*

Do you encourage your spouse to be all he or she can be? You have heard the expression that behind every good man is a good woman and that behind every good woman is a good man.

Knowing that you have the love and support of your mate is very empowering; it gives you strength and freedom. If you are not supporting your spouse properly, he or she may pull away.

If you are not supportive of your spouse, you are going against the marriage covenant and violating your marriage vows. The truth is, your marriage may not make it if you are not properly supporting each other. It takes two people to make a marriage work as God intended it.

The Biblical approach to marriage issues is to turn the situation over to God, and say, "I stand on the Word of God. If my mate takes a walk, so be it, but I am staying here in the marriage. I'm willing to learn, grow, change, and forgive." This is the position God has for every Christian in a marriage.

Unfortunately, sometimes we are so hurt emotionally that we have trouble doing this. Often, we end up as two people who are married but living separate lives.

> *Knowing that you have the love and support of your mate is very empowering; it gives you strength and freedom.*

We live in the same house, but we are not of one flesh. When you are one flesh, you are building dreams together and supporting each other. We all seem to do better when we have the security of one person's love, trust, and faithfulness. When you do not support your spouse properly, you open the door for trouble. Paul said "do not give place to the devil" (Eph. 4:27).

If your mate is looking at the opposite sex too much, then there is something wrong at home. You can blame your mate, but you need to take a look at yourself. A happy, satisfied husband or wife does not look around.

LASTING RELATIONSHIPS BEGIN WITH THE LORD

When you first get married, you go through a romantic stage. That is when you give, and you give, and you give. But when all that wears off, the real people surface. After the honeymoon is over, you may no longer think that everything your spouse does is cute.

> *We all seem to do better when we have the security of one person's love, trust, and faithfulness.*

After the newness wears off, you will see faults you never saw before. This is when you have to go back to your commitment to the Lord, even though you may feel differently about it now.

There will always be difficulties in relationships and marriages. God's plan is that you get together in prayer and work things out. You do not run away, and you don't start looking for someone else.

Consider these questions. Are you truly living up to the vows you made to each other when you were married? Do you give to your mate before you give to yourself? Do you support each other? Are you obeying God's Word in your marriage?

After the honeymoon is over, you may even think that you married the wrong person. This is why you must go back to your commitment to the Lord. After the newness wears off, you may even become bored with your spouse or tempted by someone else.

After the newness wears off, you will see faults you never saw before. This is when you have to go back to your commitment to the Lord...

But mature love is committed and does not go by feelings. Mature love is based on commitment, not on attraction. In other words, your position must be, "I am going to line up with God's Word, whether you treat me right or not, I will honor the Lord by honoring you."

Anytime there is trouble in a marriage, you must stop and closely examine your relationship with the Lord. The truth is that if you are not spending time in God's Word and in prayer, it will be difficult to love someone who has hurt you.

If you love the Lord more than your mate, then you will make it. Do not misunderstand, divorce does happen. It takes two people to make a marriage, and sometimes people do foolish things or even fail.

Sometimes people walk out of marriages when the other didn't want them to leave. You don't always have control over such matters. If this has happened to you, do not feel condemned. Recognize your own faults and ask God to bring healing into your life.

Unless you can make a new commitment to love the Lord, you will probably not be able to love your spouse in a new way. It should be noted that this applies to single people as well.

Are you willing to do whatever you have to do in order to fix that broken relationship? You can make some changes in your life, but real change can only take place through the Lord. Without God's help, serious problems and habits will not go away. But you can do all things through Christ Jesus who strengthens you (Phil. 4:13). You can change with the Lord's help.

If you desire to have better relationships with other people, then you will have to develop a deeper relationship with the Lord. You will need to "seek ye first the kingdom of God and His righteousness, and all these things shall be added to you" (Matt. 6:33).

> *After the honeymoon is over, you may even think that you married the wrong person. This is why you must go back to your commitment to the Lord.*

The "God kind" of love says, "I see your weaknesses, yet I love you anyway." The "God kind" of love says, "I will forgive by faith and trust that God will heal me of the pain I'm struggling with." It is better to forgive and patch up a broken relationship than to be right and refuse to reconcile the differences.

You may say, "But Pastor, I can't forgive them. I can't get over what they've done to me. The pain is too hard for me." You need to understand that the pain of living with an unforgiving spirit is harder than dealing with the pain of forgiving someone who has hurt you.

> Unless you can make a new commitment to love the Lord, you will probably not be able to love your spouse in a new way.

If, however, you decide not to forgive someone, then you should be aware that you are writing your own epitaph and sealing your warrant for destruction. Jesus said that if you don't forgive each other from your heart, your Heavenly Father won't forgive you or your transgressions.

If you do not like where you are, then something must change. If you keep making the same mistakes in relationships, then you need to stop running your life your way and do it God's way. Put it in the Lord's hands. It all begins with your surrender and then allowing the Lord to do a work in your heart.

It is time to take responsibility for yourself and for the direction of your life. Start taking responsibility for the mistakes you have made and stop blaming others. The real issue is not how much you have been hurt or how much you have been wounded. The issue is not whether you have been rejected. It is not what people have done to you. The issue is whether you love the Lord enough to put it all aside and "walk by faith, not by sight" (2 Cor. 5:7).

There may be times in your marriage when you feel nothing for your mate. You might even wish you were married to someone else. But since you know that God hates divorce, you must trust Him no matter what you are going through.

Of course, you do not have to put up with legitimate abuse or with adultery. But the Lord desires for you to grow to the point that you can look at your spouse and say, "I will love you no matter the cost and no matter the pain. You may not understand me, but I will love you anyway." It is about walking by faith.

When you understand that you were created for your mate and not for yourself, then you will look at your mate differently. When you understand that you are to love your spouse as Christ loved the church (Eph. 5:25), then you will forgive, even when you do not want to forgive.

In a Christian marriage, the single greatest issue is putting your spouse's needs ahead of your own for the good of the marriage.

Marriage is the testing ground for trusting God and trusting each other in spite of the glaring weaknesses each of you discover in the other.

Paul tells husbands to love their wives (Eph. 5:25). But

until you love the Lord, your God, you are not capable of loving your wife properly. And another thing: How can you love your mate unless you love yourself? The key to loving yourself and to loving your spouse is putting God first.

> It is better to forgive and patch up a broken relationship than to be right and refuse to reconcile the differences.

When you really know how much God loves you, you have the strength to love others as you love yourself. When you know that God's love has changed your life, you can become a change agent in the lives of others.

The home is supposed to be a place of comfort because life can be tough. Your family members should help carry each other's burdens and your life should be better because of the person you married. You should both be happier and live more productive lives because of your relationship. If that is not the case, then you need to seek the Lord's help with all of your heart.

One reason we see so many divorces today is because many people have erroneous ideas. Often they have bought into the belief that there is less pain and misery in "just ending the marriage and getting it over with" than there is in trusting the Lord and working to restore the relationship. They would rather go through a horrible, messy, dehumanizing divorce than to try to work things out God's way.

Such thinking reflects the hyper-individualism of our culture and is not necessarily the case, anyway. If there is going to be work and pain either way, why not allow God a chance to work in the relationship? No one is saying it's easy, and you really have to commend people who refuse to give up on their marriage, who keep hanging in there, even when they are continually let down.

Divorce is never God's way. But because of our own self-centeredness, it does take place. God's way is getting to the point that you can say, "Lord, show me how to love someone who has just hurt me," or, "God, help me pray for someone who has just been mean to me." When that happens, you can truly say that you are growing up in Jesus Christ. And when more of us can take this approach, we will see fewer divorces in the family of God and more lasting relationships built in the church of Jesus Christ.

> *In a Christian marriage, the single greatest issue is putting your spouse's needs ahead of your own for the good of the marriage.*

93

BABY, YOU ARE SO FINE

7

REAL MEN

Men need to examine their lives, their attitudes and their behavior and see how it compares to God's directives. Digging into the Bible and understanding His plan for a man's life will show men how to fight for their families.

Everyone has an image of what a real man should be like. Some people think real men are macho machines. Some people think real men look and act a certain way. But, the Bible tells us what real men are like. They are men who know who they are in Christ. Every husband and every father needs to fight for the safety of their families. Every man needs to cleanse his household with the Word of God everyday. God intends for His warriors to be the spiritual head of the family and to build up the wall of righteousness around his household through prayer and through the Word of God.

The world often portrays a man as a "ladies man." The world also often portrays a man as both rich and powerful. The world has a lot of ideas about what a man is to be like and what a man is to do. Many times these ideas have to do with how many women a man can sleep with.

However, it does not take a real man to sleep with a lot of women, but it does take a real man to stay with only one woman and defend that woman as the warrior he's been called to be. A real man puts the Lord first, above everything else in his life.

A real man stands up for righteousness, and as Joshua did, can say, "As for me and my house, we will serve the Lord" (Joshua 24:15). God's idea of a man is one who says, "There are some rules in my house, and while you're in my house, there are some things you can do and there are some things you can't."

REAL MEN
STAND AGAINST ATTACKS

Whether or not you know it, there is a spiritual enemy determined to destroy the family unit. This is why God says that men are supposed to stand and to fight for their families.

Men are usually more aggressive than women and it is their

place to stand against these attacks, and to tell the devil to get his hands off of their households. Maybe now you can understand why the enemy comes after men the way that he does.

His desire is to stop God's plan for the family. Ladies, this is why you must be determined to pray continually for your husbands. The truth is that the devil has targeted men.

When you realize that God has called men to be the head of their families, you will realize that there is a special anointing on men as the head of their households. This is why the enemy is trying to get men out of the house!

I believe Jesus came to elevate women to a position of equal rights with men. I believe Jesus came to set every captive free, including women.

This was especially true during Jesus' time when women were treated

> *Men need to examine their lives, their attitudes and their behavior and see how it compares to God's directives.*

as slaves. The Bible says that in Christ "there is neither male nor female" (Gal. 3:28), which means that God does not prefer men to women.

However, the women's movement has tried to usurp the man's authority in the home. Back in the 1960s, a unisex mentality was born. Today, we see movies with men cross-dressing and television programs that portray the man of the house as a buffoon or, at best, a weak leader. It all appears to be entertaining and funny, but what it's really all about is destroying the masculinity and the headship of the man – and the spiritual authority God has given him.

A real man stands up for righteousness, and as Joshua did, can say, "As for me and my house, we will serve the Lord" (Joshua 24:15).

Attacks can come from many different directions but they are all from the same source. The devil may aggressively get in your face or deceive you with a kiss. Whatever he tries, a real man must be ready and not back down. One attack is to get a young man to question his masculinity. God created us in His image and His image is not perverted. His image is perfect. If you are questioning your masculinity, then some type of perversion has caused you to think this way. Even if you do not feel normal, you need to line yourself up with God's Word and ask for His strength to be what He has called you to be.

Another attack is to get men so busy elsewhere that there is no time to spiritually lead their families. Because men are not leading, women have to step into that role. This has put things out of order.

The Bible is very clear that the home was designed with men as the spiritual leaders and when they don't lead, there will be trouble in the household.

The world tries to portray Godly men as weak. This is another spiritual attack by the enemy. If you think it is "weak" to serve the Lord, then you need to know it takes a real man to stand up in the face of criticism and say, "As for me and my house, we will serve the Lord" (Josh. 24:15). Men are called to stand up against attacks and lead the family by example. God did not call men to be dictators, but to lovingly lead. Do your children see you preaching one thing and doing another? Does your wife see you praying? Do you drop your family off for church or do you lead by example? It takes a real man to bring his family to church and to serve the Lord.

> *When you realize that God has called men to be the head of their families, you will realize that there is a special anointing on men as the head of their households.*

As a man, you have more influence over your home than you realize. Your family is going to follow your lead. Does your family see you tithing on a regular basis?

Some men spend their money on just about anything except the gospel of Jesus Christ. What example are you setting? Do you spend your money on things for you while your family does without? Your children will follow your example!

And, your example will lead them to heaven or to hell. That is an awesome responsibility, but it is the truth. Maybe now you can understand why the male is under such attack. If the enemy can cut off the head, then the family will die. You need to be a real man, and you need to stand up for righteousness.

Real Men Fulfill Obligations

> *Attacks can come from many different directions but they are all from the same source.*

The majority of our youth today live in a home where the mother has taken the leadership role. Over half of the youth in America live in a single-parent home that is headed by a woman.

You can be the best mom in the world, but without a Godly man in leadership, there will be trouble in the home. It's no wonder kids are on drugs. It's no wonder drug use has doubled in the last three years among teens – and that the average age of children having sex is thirteen.

The main reason gangs are flourishing today is because children do not have a real family at home, and they're creating their own families. Many of these children have an absent father or they do not know who their father is.

Many homes have a father, but he's not involved in his children's lives. There is something about a father's love that brings stability. It's no wonder the family unit is endangered today.

When children do not receive male approval at home, they will seek it in other ways, even if these ways are perverted. They need to know "the wages of sin is death" (Romans 6:23). The truth is that your sin will find you out. Your sin will destroy you!

When men are in their rightful place, there is a protection over the entire home. As a man, you need to know that there is a spiritual enemy who is threatening your home right now. The Lord is calling you to lead your family in the paths of righteousness.

> *The Bible is very clear that the home was designed with men as the spiritual leaders and when they don't lead, there will be trouble in the household.*

When Moses told the tribes of Reuben and Gad to build homes for their families and barns for their livestock, he was telling them to provide security for them as the number one obligation, and then come and fight for God's kingdom. In other words, before they could save the world, they needed to secure their homes. We need men today to catch this vision and this sense of order.

The enemy fights hard against men and their spiritual leadership. For example, the life expectancy of males is seven years less than females. We are told that 90% of all violent crimes are committed by men; 75% of all suicides in America are by men; and 94% of all drunk drivers are men. Men are 25 times more likely to be committed to a mental institution than women are. This is all a wicked strategy the enemy has planned against men and their spiritual leadership.

The enemy has particularly targeted the black man. His plan is to kill the head of the family and to try and destroy the leadership of his home. In general, black people are more in tune with the spiritual realm. Our spiritual enemy obviously recognizes the great potential of the black man or he wouldn't be fighting him so hard.

It is time for men — black, brown, white, of whatever color, to ban together and fight the enemy. It is time for us to pray over our homes together and to believe God will provide for our families, "because He who is in you is greater than he who is in the world" (I John 4:4).

The disease AIDS is also about killing males. It's interesting how the devil tried to kill all male children at the time of Moses' birth because he was afraid of male leadership and the male babies of Bethlehem at the birth of Jesus Christ.

The enemy is still doing everything he can to destroy men and their families, because the family is the primary source of love, strength and stability. Whenever the father is not in his place, the family and society is in big trouble.

REAL MEN LEAD

The word "husband" means "house band." It is the husband who is to band the house together. It is the husband who is supposed to stand up for righteousness and say, "Hey, devil, get your hands off my children! Get your hands off my wife!" It is the husband who is to train the children in the ways of the Lord.

> The main reason gangs are flourishing today is because children do not have a real family at home, and they're creating their own families.

Any male can produce a child, but it takes a real man to lead his family in the ways of the Lord. Any male can get a female pregnant, but it takes a real man to be a father who will get involved with his children. Any male can be married, but it takes a real man to get up early in the morning and to spiritually wash his family in the water of the Word.

It takes a real man to lay hands on his family and pray over their healing. It takes a real man to discipline his children instead of leaving it up to their mother.

If the mother is the one who does all the disciplining, then children do not learn to respect the authority of men. Men, if you do not learn to discipline your children, the police will do it for you! If you do not learn to band your house together, then your children will be loose on the streets, and there is no telling what they will do.

Every child needs male leadership and male role models. Unfortunately, we live in a world today where most of our role models are athletes, and most of them set terrible examples. That's why male leadership is so important in the church and so important in our schools.

Some children have no male leadership around them and we must do everything possible — as a church and as a community — to bring male leadership into our children's lives.

Women are leading their families because men have let them down. Women are frankly fed up because men will not take their rightful place.

Let me say it this way: Women are mad because men will not do what they are supposed to do! If you were to ask the average Christian woman what is the most important thing in her marriage, I believe the majority would say for her husband to take his rightful place as the spiritual head and the spiritual leader of the family.

If you were to ask the average single Christian woman what she wants most in a man, I believe she would say, "For a man who is not afraid to be a Godly man."

Maybe those of you who are women can now understand why you're not to be unequally yoked. If the man you're dating is not sold out to the Lord, you are going to have a mess on your hands before everything is over! And, believe me, you are not going to change him either.

You also need to know that you can both be saved and still be unequally yoked. He may be a Christian, but he may never be at your level of Godliness. When this happens it is often impossible for him to lead. That's why the dating process is so important. It is in the courting process that you learn what kind of man you have.

Take a lesson from the courting process of the eagles. When the male eagle begins to court the female, she'll take a stick and fly up to a certain elevation and drop the stick, and then see if the male can catch it before it hits the ground.

> It is time for men — black, brown, white, of whatever race, to ban together and fight the devil.

She will pick up bigger sticks and fly lower to the ground and keep dropping them to see if the male can continue to catch them before they hit the ground.

If a stick ever hits earth, the courtship is over. She is trying to find out whether or not the male will be a good provider. She is trying to find out if this guy can band their house together!

Unfortunately, most women will take the first joker that comes along, especially Christian women. Sister, let me tell you something, you can do bad all by yourself. You don't need some no good, lay up in the bed all day, can't get a job, can I have your car keys man messing up your life. Now that's the only way I know how to say that.

> *Any male can produce a child, but it takes a real man to lead his family in the ways of the Lord.*

If he's been married before, find out if he is taking care of his children now. Find out if he pays his bills. The Bible says, "he who finds a wife finds a good thing" (Proverbs 18:22). Women, you are not to be looking for a husband. Men are to look for you! You are to be busy working for the Lord and trust Him to find you what you need.

It is God's plan that you make Jesus the man in your life. It is God's plan that you tell all the girls at work that you have a new man who treats you better than you treat yourself.

It is God's plan that you seek Him first, and that you let Him bring a good Godly gift into your life.

REAL MEN ARE GODLY

The Bible makes it very clear how we are to live our lives as Godly men. The bottom line is that the Lord must be first in all things. A Godly man is committed to one woman, the woman he's married to, and he does not sleep around with other women.

A Godly man accepts responsibility. A Godly man is honest; he tells the truth and he does not lie. A Godly man makes a commitment and then he follows through with that commitment.

A Godly man is hard working because God blesses the work of his hands. If you are not working, then God will not bless you! A Godly man is forgiving. A Godly man protects his family. A Godly man is humble, and he says, "I am sorry."

This is what the meeting between Moses and the men of Israel was all about. Moses was making Godly men out of all of them. If the two tribes wanted to live on the opposite bank of the Jordan, that was well within God's plan as long as they followed through with their commitment to conquer the Promised Land with the rest of the troops.

Convenience could not triumph over consecration. Moses had spent forty years building men set aside for God's purposes, and he was not going to let a choice of real estate destroy those forty years. The devil was ready to ruin the mission, but Moses quickly acted to get the work moving in the right direction again.

Since God made man to work, then men ought to dive right in and be the best provider and protector he possibly can be. It is God who set the man as the head of the family. If a man refuses to accept the spiritual responsibility of being the head of the family, then that man is refusing to be obedient to the Lord.

If a man does not submit to his role as the head of the family, then that man is fighting God. If you as a woman marry someone you can't submit to, then you are going to be in trouble. A Godly woman will have no problem submitting to a man who is properly submitted to the Lord.

Men, if you will submit to the Lord in every area of your life, you will probably find your wife submitting to you in a wonderful new way.

Ladies, you have to let your man lead. If you will step out of the leadership role, then he'll have no choice but to lead. Even if he makes a lot of mistakes, you have to let him lead. If you do not, you are fighting God's plan for your household.

God always intended for the man to be the *house band*, and not the wife. God intended for the man to be the one who provided the house – the shelter and protection – for the family. Though society has changed, God never intended for a woman to be in the work place and to be the one responsible for providing for her family.

Today's women are often forced to compete in the workplace and struggle to provide for their families. Women are experiencing the pressures of finances when God designed men to be the *house band*s and providers.

God made man to be the giver. He gives his wife a house and she makes it a home. Husbands, are you a giver to your wife? Do you spend more money on her or on yourself? Are you taking care of her properly? Does the ring on her finger, her clothes or her car tell everybody how much you love her?

When a young Jewish man became engaged to a young Jewish woman, he would say to her, "I go to prepare a place for you." Under Jewish law, a young man could not marry a Jewish woman until he could give her a house.

When men rise up in their families and take their rightful place, the enemy is defeated. When men rise up in the church and take their rightful place, the enemy is defeated again.

> *A Godly man is committed to one woman, the woman he's married to...*

Churches that have proper male leadership are churches that are strong. We believe women are equal with men in the church. We believe in women in the ministry. But, we also believe that men are to take their rightful place in leadership and headship.

God says He is looking for men willing to build up the wall of righteousness and stand in the gap for those who need help (Eze. 22:30). God is also looking for men willing to build walls of righteousness around their households and their churches so destruction will not take place.

As a man, you must be determined to say, "Hey devil, get your hands off my family in Jesus' Name!" Every once in a while you must stand up and say, "As for me and my house, we will serve the Lord" (Josh.24:15).

If your family is in trouble, it could have something to do with you, the husband, not "banding" the house together. If there is a problem in your marriage, then you need to seek the Lord, put Him first, and ask for His help.

It's time for men to take their rightful place as leaders. It's time to be a Real Man!

8

REAL WOMEN

Let's head back to the Garden of Eden as we look at the calling women have upon their lives. When the serpent came into the garden to destroy what God had created, he headed straight for the woman, Eve, with the temptation. "Did God really say you shouldn't eat from any of the trees in this beautiful garden?" he asked her.

Here was a test concerning contentment. The devil started with an overstatement to hide the real issue, which was eating from the *one* tree from which God told them not to eat.

Satan was using an emotional ploy to get man and woman to fall from God's grace. When Eve answered the serpent she also overstated God's orders to make her case, "We can eat from all the trees in the garden but not from the tree in the center. If we eat from that tree, *or even touch its fruit*, we will die!" Eve's overstatement was the beginning of the downfall.

God had not told Adam and Eve not to touch the fruit. He told them not to eat of the fruit. By not following God's Word, Eve opened herself to doubt.

Next, when the devil informed Eve that she would not die but become like God, she picked some fruit and held it in her hand and she did not die (Gen. 3:6).

Now there was real doubt in Eve's mind as to what to believe. She held the fruit, looked at it, and since it was so desirable, she took a bite of the forbidden fruit and ate it. But here's the incredible part about the fall: Eve then took the fruit and gave some to her husband "who was with her, and he ate it" (Gen. 3:6).

The grammatical construction of this statement in the Hebrew text makes it very possible that Adam was with Eve while she was being tempted and did nothing to stop what was happening. If this is true, then every time we look at the characteristics that distinguish men and women, we must determine whether they are God-intended or a ploy by the devil to interfere with God's plan. Satan set up Eve to fall, and he did it right in front of the man.

To aid his deception in the Garden of Eden, satan tried to

manipulate every aspect of the woman's personality, and the world is doing the same thing today.

Could this possibly be connected with the enemy again? In the same manner, every aspect of the man's personality was under attack in the Garden, and it still is today.

Men are being told to please themselves, and to do whatever it takes to keep peace in the family even if it means compromise. They're advised to take chances and to not make judgements about moral issues and to be more open-minded.

When you think of a real woman, what comes to mind? Do you think of physical characteristics such as how tall she is or what she looks like? When the world portrays a woman, it usually depicts someone who drinks a certain kind of booze or someone who smokes a certain brand of cigarettes.

> *Men are being told to please themselves, and to do whatever it takes to keep peace in the family even if it means compromise.*

To the world, a real woman has a lot of sex appeal and she dresses in ways that show it. She will probably look terrific in a bikini and may be a player in the bars from time to time.

The world says that a woman is a seductive temptress, someone who has a certain type of build, shows her cleavage and knows how to wiggle certain parts of her body when she walks. To the world, a woman is someone who is self-sufficient.

She has come a long way. A real woman can serve in the army and can do almost anything that a man can. She doesn't need a man because she is a leader herself. This is the very picture we are given when Eve met the serpent in the Garden. This is the very personality satan set up. He approached her instead of Adam when it was time to get mankind to fall.

The world says that a woman is a seductive temptress, someone who has a certain type of build...

The Bible's perspective of how a Godly woman is supposed to be is; she is totally submitted to the Lord above everything else, she is spiritual and a teacher of spiritual things to her family. A Godly woman is in submission to her husband (Eph. 5:22-23).

She is supportive of her husband, and she is so smart that she is able to make decisions for the family and make her husband think it was his idea.

Let's go back to the Garden to understand this "submission" issue a little better.

God created Adam from the dust of the earth, and Adam walked this planet for some time before it was decided he needed a helper. When the time did come for a partner to be created for Adam, it was from man that God created Eve.

Now understand what has happened here; Adam was a part of the earth, but Eve was a part of man. This is why men receive their self-esteem mostly from their work while women receive their self-esteem mostly from their man.

She is supportive of her husband, and she is so smart that she is able to make decisions for the family and make her husband think it was his idea.

This is not an issue of being better, this is an issue of God's design and purpose for His creation. He created man specifically for the purpose He assigned to man. God also created women specifically for the purpose He assigned to woman.

This is why a Godly woman understands that, in Christ, the male is not better than the female. She knows Jesus came to set every captive free, including women.

But she also knows that her husband is the head of the house by God's design, and she will not fight this plan but will work within these parameters.

REAL WOMEN FOLLOW GOD

What is a real woman? She is someone who is sold out to the Lord, and then to her family. Her husband never has to worry whether or not she will be faithful to him.

While the world says that you can have sex with whomever you want, God says that a Godly woman loves the Lord so much that she would never consider having sex with anyone except her husband. Temptations may come across her mind, but she takes "every thought captive to the obedience of Christ" (2 Cor. 10:5). She is submitted first to God. This is why a man needs to find a woman who loves God more than she loves anything else in her life.

> *What is a real woman? She is someone who is sold out to the Lord, and then to her family.*

A Godly woman treats her husband as though he is her knight in shining armor. She gives her opinions and then allows him make his own decisions. This may mean she also allows him to make his own mistakes.

Above all, she respects and admires her man because respect gives him power. Paul said in Ephesians 5:33, "Let the wife see that she respects her husband." You may have to do this by faith, especially if your husband is not living for the Lord.

A Godly woman knows how fragile the male ego is. She continually builds up her husband and makes him think he is good at everything he does.

A woman must know when to give her husband suggestions and when to back off. You have to know when to give your opinion and when to be quiet.

Men and women do not think the same way. For example, when women get upset they want to talk. Whereas when men get upset, they're silent and want to be left alone.

Statistics show that women speak an average of 25,000 words a day and men only speak an average of 12,000 words a day. Women want to talk and communicate. They love to give advice. Sometimes you need to be patient and your husband will come around. Give him your advice and then let him do it his way. Do not ask him to carve the turkey and then tell him how to do it.

The Word says it is "better to dwell in a corner of a housetop, than in a house shared with a contentious woman" (Prov. 21:9). The Bible says a Godly woman is never quarrelsome, but is submitted to her husband (Eph. 5:22).

In other words, she has learned to pray and to give up control to God. She does not quarrel with her husband's decisions because she trusts the Lord more than she trusts her husband.

REAL WOMEN ARE SUBMISSIVE

Perhaps you think that God's command to submit means you are not as important or intelligent as your husband. But, a Godly woman knows that when she is submitted to her husband she is also honoring the Lord.

A Godly woman knows that if she honors the Lord properly, blessings will eventually come. It takes a Godly woman to submit to an unreasonable man. In fact, it takes humility to be a submissive wife.

We live in a very rebellious time. People do not want to be told how to live their lives. The truth is that women can do very well without men in their lives. However, God has called the man to lead his family and the wife to be his helper.

> *A godly woman knows that if she honors the Lord properly, blessings will eventually come*

Every football team has a quarterback, but where would the quarterback be unless he had people blocking for him? Where would he be if the team did not support him?

The same principle applies to the man of the house. If you do not support and pray for him, how can he possibly be successful? If you have an abusive past, or if you had an absentee father, it may be difficult for you to be submissive. But, you can do all things through Christ who strengthens you (Phil. 4:13).

Just because your mother was overbearing and domineering does not mean you have to be. Just because your grandmother was a controller does not mean you have to be. Also, if your husband is not saved, it is a whole lot easier to win him to the Lord by being submissive than by being rebellious. When you show your unsaved husband a submissive attitude, he will no longer be threatened by Jesus.

There is something about men that makes them need to be in control. In fact, the reason your husband does not want you going to church all the time is because he sees himself losing control. He can see that when Jesus is Lord, he is no longer your lord.

You must be careful about how you handle this issue of control. Do not put the church before your husband. Do not neglect your husband in order to listen to tapes or even to serve in the church. If you do, then he is likely to feel resentment.

This does not mean you do not have a life of your own. But, if the Lord shows you an area where you are missing the mark, then do something about it. If God shows you some changes you need to make, then make those changes.

REAL WOMEN BUILD GOD'S WAY

When God says to be subject to one another, He is telling us to be servant builders. The ideal situation would be for you and your husband to pray over everything and make decisions together. But, when God says to be subject to one another, He is also saying to prefer the other person over yourself.

> ...if the Lord shows you an area where you are missing the mark, then do something about it. If God shows you some changes you need to make, then make those changes.

When you made your wedding vows, you gave up your will in order to become one flesh with a single purpose. Love is never enough to hold two people together. But, if you are truly one flesh and have a single purpose, you will have enough to stay together. The problem with a two-career household is that you can become roommates instead of help-meets. God has called you to help meet the needs of your spouse.

Marriage is about serving, building a new life together and supporting each other.

God's plan for a wife is for her to love, respect and admire her husband so much that he cannot resist her. If your man does not feel as though you admire, respect and support him, he will build walls around himself and shut you out. When you stand behind him, he hears love. When you constantly criticize him, he hears that he is not good enough. This is why you should never criticize your husband in front of others. A softer approach is always better.

You, the woman, are so important to the family that if you do not learn to encourage your husband, he may not do very well in life. He may not do well on the job, in financial matters or in your marriage.

If he feels a lack of support, he will shut you out of his life. If he shuts you out, there will be no communication, no love, and he will become a workaholic in order to avoid you. A real woman will empower her husband with strength because of the way she supports him.

The secret to empowering a man is to never try to change him and to never try to improve him. You need to pray for him, encourage him, build him up, admire him and respect him and allow God to work through him.

> *When God says to be subject to one another, He is telling us to be servant builders.*

When you use an impatient or demanding voice, your man can no longer hear you, it doesn't matter what you are requesting. What he hears is that he is not good enough and he is tired of hearing someone, like his mother, nagging him.

You may say, "Well pastor, what is a wife supposed to do when her husband is an unloving, unreasonable tyrant? What is a woman supposed to do if a man is so stingy that he never gives?" Then you need to have a "you and me" talk, a confrontation in love, but this should not be done in anger; otherwise he will not hear you.

REAL WOMEN PRAY

The secret to empowering a man is to never try to change him and to never try to improve him. You need to pray for him, encourage him...

A real woman is one who puts the Lord first and then takes care of her family. She is a good example to others. She dresses with good taste and class. She is kind in speech, forgiving, and not a gossip, trustworthy and nurturing. She is a lady, and she is a prayer warrior.

Men, if you are thinking about marrying a woman who has been married before, find out how she treated her last husband. If she has children, find out how she treats her kids.

Find out whether she is a hard worker or is she lazy. For you ladies, the question is, are you a real woman by God's standards or a real woman by the world's standards? Do you support your partner's goals and dreams? Do you encourage or discourage? Are you committed to your spouse no matter what?

Marriage is not so much about finding love or even finding a perfect mate. It is about giving and meeting the other person's needs. It is about being a real woman according to God's standards.

If you are born again, then you believe divorce is wrong and should never happen. However, if you are not one with your spouse, if you do not encourage and support them, then your baggage may be heavier than what they may be able to carry.

When a man or a woman has a mid-life crisis, it usually has to do with not being admired, or respected, not being encouraged and feeling trapped. And whether or not men will admit it, nothing is as important as a good sex life.

It is important to keep a clean house and to care for the kids, but nothing compares to sexual fulfillment. Now that you are born-again, you need to know that your body belongs to your husband (1 Cor. 7:4). Because you are submitted to God's Word, you are to never withhold sex as a form of control.

Women need to know that sexual frustration for a man can lead to great bitterness and anger. If you are withholding sex, then you are out of God's order. A sexually satisfied husband is usually happier, a better provider, more thoughtful and stronger emotionally.

Do not ever underestimate the importance of your supportive role. Sometimes, men have the attitude that they don't need anyone, but the truth is, men need women more than women need men.

Husbands and wives should learn to dress for each other. Husbands, you should not criticize your wife's clothes unless you are willing to buy her new ones. Ladies, learn to dress for your man. Wear what he likes, and be attractive for him.

Men, if you are thinking about marrying a woman who has been married before, find out how she treated her last husband.

One of the biggest complaints I hear from men is that their wife took time making sure she looked good for him before they married, and today she's totally let herself go; overweight, no makeup, doesn't do her hair, totally inactive, and doesn't exercise.

Now on the other hand, the women might respond to that and say, "Well, I have to take care of the kids, run them here for this activity, run them there for that. I work outside of the home, besides, cook, clean and run the washing machine!" So when do I have time for myself?

You and your spouse need to sit down together and evaluate your needs , prioritize them and then set a plan on how those things are going to get accomplished. If you want your wife to exercise and lose weight, then you watch the kids in the evening while she goes to the gym. Or better still, hire a baby-sitter to watch the kids and you go with her since you probably aren't exactly prince charming today either.

If you are a Godly woman, then you will learn to become a prayer warrior and put things into God's hands. Whether or not you know it, the devil is after your man, and it is his plan to destroy him. It is your prayers that will cause your man to make it.

Are you a Godly woman? Then you are a hard worker (Prov. 31:10-33). Whether you work inside or outside of the home, you are not lazy. A Godly woman is very wise with the family money because she saves and follows a budget. When she makes her own money, she invests it wisely. She

When a man or a woman has a mid-life crisis, it usually has to do with not being admired, or respected, not being encouraged...

is not a "gold digger" who has to live off of a man. She doesn't need to have a man take care of her because she works hard and plans ahead.

The Bible says that a Godly woman is compassionate, always reaching out to the poor and needy (Prov. 31:20). She is very loving and giving. She is never idle and works as hard as her husband works. The end result is that she is greatly praised (Prov. 31:30-31).

One of the greatest attributes of a Godly woman is that she is humble. A real woman will learn to say, "I'm sorry," because it takes humility to do so. She does not fight for position, but instead prays and trusts in the Lord.

Most of all, a Godly woman knows that she plays a supportive role in the Christian family. She understands that she is the helper who can cause her family to win. She is so smart that she is the neck that turns the head of the family.

> *You and your spouse need to sit down together and evaluate your needs, prioritize them and then set a plan...*

God's order for the home cannot be accomplished without strong women, yielding themselves to fit into the role God has created them for.

9

THE POWER OF AGREEMENT

Because the battles that Christians face are spiritual ones, one of the biggest obstacles in the way of getting your house in order is your spiritual enemy. Just when you think you have your heart, your life, your family and your relationships in order, the enemy attacks you.

Your spiritual enemy will constantly attack you individually, attack your marriage, attack your family, and attack every aspect of your life, including your walk with the Lord. His plan is to isolate you and to prevent you from coming into agreement with your spouse, your children, your friends, and other believers.

All relationships carry the potential for strife. Whether

it's in your marriage or within your family, with church members, with significant others if you are single, with friends or people with whom you work, there is always the possibility of conflict. The devil knows that a house divided cannot stand (Matt. 12:25), thus he will do everything that he can to cause strife and to keep strife in your relationships. If you are going to get your house in order, then you must get the strife out of your life. You must get into God's Word and do what God says.

> *Wholeness comes from within, not from someone else. It comes by putting the Lord first in your life.*

The Bible says that when people come together in unity, a real anointing comes upon them (Psa. 133). When people are one in the spirit, the anointing will fall. As long as people are bickering and fighting, the devil does not have to worry about us. As long as we are arguing among ourselves, your spiritual enemy can sit back and laugh because he knows he will win.

We need a fresh anointing in our lives so that we can see miracles take place. We need a fresh touch of the Holy Ghost so we can see miracles working through us. This is why we cannot afford to allow strife or division in our lives. One of the keys to the anointing is getting all divisive conflicts behind us. There is something about bickering and fighting that stops the power of God from working. Paul prayed that there would be no divisions among us (Eph. 4:31). He knew that divisions would stop the presence of God from working. It is not worthwhile to win an argument if it causes strife and division because you'll end up losing more than you gained.

Understand that your spiritual enemy understands the power of agreement and he wants to keep this power from coming into your life and into your relationships. You need this power of agreement if you are going to get your house in order.

Whether you are single or married, you need to learn to be married to the Lord first. If you are married to the Lord, then you can be happy regardless of your

> *It is very important that you learn about loving God so that you can eventually learn to love who you are.*

circumstances. If you are single, then you can give yourself totally to the Lord without having to answer to a spouse.

You can pursue goals and dreams without someone restricting you. That's important because you need to learn to enjoy every stage of your life otherwise you may have trouble letting go of one stage and moving on to the next.

For example, if you did not enjoy your childhood, then you will probably grow up being childish. If you did not enjoy being single, then you will probably get married and wish that you were single again. So, learn to celebrate life right now whatever your situation, and stop looking for someone else to make you happy.

> *If you are not happy being alone, then you will continually look to others for your happiness.*

Wholeness comes from within, not from someone else. It comes by putting the Lord first in your life. If you marry someone thinking that they will make you complete, there will be trouble because no person can bring you wholeness. If you are waiting for someone to come into your life so that you can be happy, then you'll probably be waiting a long time. You need to learn to be happy now or you will always look to some**thing** or some**one** for happiness. If you are not careful, you will miss what God has for you.

Paul said, "Not that I speak in regard to need, for I have learned in whatever state I am, to be content" (Phil. 4:11). It does not matter whether you are single, married, rich, or poor, you need to be happy where you are.

Jesus said that the greatest commandment was, "to love the Lord your God with all your heart" (Mark 12:30). Then He said, "You shall love your neighbor as yourself" (Mark 12:31). It is very important that you understand about loving God so that you can eventually learn to love who you are.

Once you like yourself, then it is easy to like your neighbor. But, until you learn to love God, you cannot even like yourself. If you do not like yourself, then you cannot like other people.

LOOK TO THE LORD FOR HEALING

As you go through life, people will hurt you and stuff will happen to you. Because of the pain and feelings of rejection, you will tend to build walls around yourself and then hide behind these walls.

You are not going to have renewed strength by waiting on a person. Strength comes from waiting on the Lord.

This, however, will bring unhappiness into your life. You must develop a mentality of being happy by yourself before you can be happy with someone else. If you are not happy being alone, then you will continually look to others for your happiness.

There is nothing more draining than being in a relationship in which one person cannot be happy without the constant presence of the other. If you've ever experienced it, you know how completely exhausting and draining a relationship can be if you have someone clinging to you for his or her happiness.

You can't be totally available for someone else, and no one can be there for you all of the time. God never intended for one person to meet all of our needs. Our needs are to be met through dependence on the Lord Jesus Christ. It is God's plan to "supply all your need according to His riches in glory by Christ Jesus" (Phil. 4:19). Those who wait on the Lord shall renew their strength" (Isa. 40:31).

> *No doubt you have been hurt in the past, but you can never build a future until you let it go, until you forgive, and until you allow God do a new work in you.*

You are not going to have renewed strength by waiting on a person. Strength comes from waiting on the Lord. Stop looking to people to make you happy and start looking to the Lord.

Needy people will drain the life out of you. Your husband cannot be your God. Your wife cannot be your God. Your boyfriend or your girlfriend cannot be your God. In fact, if you are not careful, you will drain the life out of those around you because you are so needy yourself.

For example, when you are not whole and your mate tells you he or she needs time alone, you may take it as rejection and feel that your spouse isn't loving you adequately. In reality, you may need for God to heal you so that your spouse can feel that he or she has a true partner – rather than a leech hanging on for dear life.

It is interesting that we are often attracted to people who have the same weaknesses we have. This is why unhealthy people are attracted to other unhealthy people and whole people are attracted to whole people.

The real problem is that because we are unhealthy in some area of our lives, we tend to pick people who are just like us. Then, we blame them for our problems, and because we both have similar baggage, life seems to be a war zone. We are always in battles.

Because of all of the hurts in our past, we now put up walls in order to protect ourselves. But, the problem is that the walls are isolating us and creating more pain. No doubt you have been hurt in the past, but you can never build a future until you let it go, until you forgive, and until you allow God to do a new work in you.

BAGGAGE CAUSES PROBLEMS

The reason that people keep going from relationship to relationship is because they are not healthy enough to work things out. They are going through life blaming everybody else for their miserable life.

If this describes you, it is time for you to look at yourself and say, "God, fix me." One of the main reasons it is so important to go through premarital counseling is because when you marry someone, you are marrying everything they have gone through. You are married to any abuse they may have experienced. You are married to all of the good and all of the bad of the past. You are married to all of their generational blessings and curses.

> *If you are defensive, it is probably because of the way that a previous partner treated you...*

When you get married, this bonding includes both families. You may think that you are not marrying their family, but in reality you are. You bring all of someone's past into your life when you marry.

If you do not deal with it now, you will have to deal with it later. Unfortunately, we treat our mates in certain ways because of our pasts. If you are defensive, it is probably because of the way that a previous partner treated you; consequently, you are determined that nobody is ever going to treat you that way again.

And, you are determined that nobody is ever going to do to you what someone else did. You are causing the new partner to "pay" for the emotional debt the previous partner left you with. The problem is you are carrying all of this baggage with you, and it is preventing you from building a healthy relationship.

The real reason you cannot build a great relationship with your partner is because you will not leave the things of the past behind. God said that the two of you shall become one flesh as you leave your parents and as you cleave to [*cling to*] each other.

If you do not leave these things behind, if you do not get healed of them, you will end up making your spouse pay for everything someone else did to you.

The Bible states that a man is to leave his mother and father and cleave to his wife (Eph. 5:31). That means the couple is to start a new family unit. Cleaving to each other means breaking the old patterns of dependence upon the family of childhood and establishing new adult patterns of interdependence within the new family unit – you and your spouse.

When you are married, you have to leave some things behind or you cannot truly cleave to each other. Before you can cleave to one another, you have to let some things go. You have to leave some hurts behind, you have to leave some walls and barriers behind, and you have to leave some parents behind. You have to leave childhood behind and grow up.

You have to get to the point where you leave these things

and reach forward to what lies ahead. You have to get over the things your mother did, or what your dad did to your mother, or what your dad did to you, or even the fact that he was not there for you.

> *If you are going to have a successful marriage, then your partner must know that you have his or her back covered.*

If you do not leave these things behind, if you do not get healed of them, you will end up making your spouse pay for everything someone else did to you. Your spouse will be a constant hostage in the marriage. If you do not leave your past behind, then you cannot cleave to someone else.

It is amazing how your past can be killing you, yet you still hang on to it. It is amazing how your past can tear up relationships, but you refuse to turn it loose. The reason is because you are wounded and feel abused, used, or treated unfairly. That's why you have the anger issues that you have. You are angry because you are hurting. You may want justice and to clear your name. You may want others to acknowledge that you were wronged, and so on.

And, you may be right. But hanging on to those things is the wrong way to get what you are seeking. You need to forgive and forget, to leave behind those things in the past, and move on.

If you are going to have a successful marriage, then your partner must know that you have his or her back covered. Therefore, you should not divulge what your partner tells you in confidence or use those things to control their behavior. That's emotional blackmail and extremely cruel and juvenile. Your partner needs to know that you are his or her number one supporter and number one fan and that no matter what happens, you will not leave.

You will never have a great marriage until you learn to communicate and to talk to each other, not at each other. Communication helps you to get to the heart of the matter and discover the real issues. But, often we really do not communicate because we are too prideful to tell it like it is. We do not want people to know how insecure we really are.

> When people have unmet needs they may fight and squabble about one thing, when actually something else is the real problem.

Many times the reason that people do not communicate how they feel with others is because whenever they try, they are criticized and told they shouldn't feel that way rather than listened to and encouraged.

So, rather than try to communicate with others, they just clam up and give people the silent treatment. If you're having trouble communicating with others, perhaps they've turned you off for this reason.

Remember, people do not need someone to act like their dad or their mom. They need you to listen to them quietly, so they can tell you how they really feel without being condemned.

When people have unmet needs, they may fight and squabble about one thing, when actually something else is the real problem.

> ...being in agreement with others requires self-knowledge and the humility to admit your weaknesses...

For example, you may yell at your spouse for not putting the top on the toothpaste, but, in reality, you may be irritated and feel you are not getting what you need emotionally, perhaps appreciation.

Such misplaced anger arises from a general sense of unhappiness or frustration. It is not a conscious decision to mislead others, but the result of the actor being misled by his or her own emotions. If you are unaware of what is really bothering you, you may become mad and yell about the toothpaste. Thus, being in agreement with others requires self-knowledge and the humility to admit your weaknesses and your needs and is crucial to healthy relationships.

How many times do we struggle with jealousy, but do not like to admit it because we are not supposed to be jealous? How many times do we struggle with insecurity, but we are too insecure to talk about it?

Most of us are too proud to say, "Lord I am hurting and I need Your help. My life is a mess and I need Your healing. Lord, help me to overcome my past." How many times do we struggle with life's issues, but we do not talk about it? These are the real issues we must deal with if we are going to cleave to each other and avoid emotional distancing.

WHAT IS MARRIAGE?

Some people spend their whole lives looking for "the right person." If you pray and seek God's help, there is someone who will fit you perfectly. With God's help, you can build a great life together. This is why marriage is not so much about sex, or love, or finding the right person, it is about being committed to meeting the other person's needs and about supporting your partner's goals and dreams.

Marriage is about each partner encouraging the other to be all that he or she can be. It is about building confidence in one another, about being a team, about supporting each other, about becoming one flesh, and about building intimacy.

There is no such thing as a perfect mate. Marriage is spending your life with your best friend and sharing your life with someone you completely trust. It is about mutual love, mutual respect, and mutual nurturing.

However, because we are so needy, we jump into bed with the first person that comes along and gives us any attention.

> *You cannot change where you have been, but you can change where you are going. It is time to stop criticizing each other...*

We just jump right into bed without thinking about a friendship or what God says about it. You do not build friendships through sex. In fact, sex will mess up a friendship.

One of the most important ingredients in a happy marriage is the friendship between the two of you – you are, or should be, best friends. If you are married to your best friend, then you can weather any storm that comes your way. If your spouse is not your best friend, then you need to open the communication in order to establish a true friendship.

You need to communicate freely and openly and you need to understand each other. The two of you need to go to dinner and talk things out regularly.

It is important for men to be careful of their tone of voice. Men, it is not what you say, but how you say it. Attacking each other will do no good. The answer is cleaving to one another.

You cannot change where you have been, but you can

change where you are going. It is time to stop criticizing each other, bury the past, leave some things behind, and drop the charges that you have against each other.

You will never have the anointing of God in your house as long as you are fighting each other. If you want to see the anointing of God on your family, then there must be unity. There must be unity between the parents, between the parents and the children, and between the children.

God tells us that we are to take spiritual dominion wherever we go. We are to spiritually rule and reign on this earth together. "We do not wrestle against flesh and blood, but against principalities, against powers, against rulers of the darkness of this age, against spiritual hosts of wickedness in the heavenly places" (Eph. 6:12).

> *You need to make up your mind that fromthis day forward your home is going to be a place of peace and safety.*

Our fight is not with our parents or our spouses. Our fight is with our spiritual enemy. You cannot have a happy home until you learn to stop fighting each other and start fighting the devil.

You need to make up your mind that from this day forward your home is going to be a place of peace and safety. From this day forward, be determined that your home is a no war zone and stop fighting.

It is time to get some things turned around in your relationship. It is time to forget the past and press towards a new beginning. You need to turn your guns on the devil, not your family.

There are some things you cannot get accomplished by yourself. You need the power of agreement to change your family. The devil is in trouble when your family is in agreement. It is time to gang up on the devil.

This is why you must learn to praise each other and not criticize. Men listen, God's Word says that if you criticize your wife, He will not hear your prayers (1 Peter 3:7). If you speak against your wife, your prayers go unanswered. As long as you are mean to your wife, God says He will shut the doors around you.

As long as you are bickering and fighting with your wife, nothing is going to work out for you. Your prayers will not be answered until there is love, respect, and unity.

If you expect God's help in your life, then you need to learn to get that piece of your life turned around. You must learn "that if two of you agree on earth concerning anything that they ask, it will be done for them by My Father in heaven" (Matt. 18:19). The reason your spiritual enemy loves it when you fight is because he knows the power generated when people come into agreement. When a married couple agree together, the devil knows he is in big trouble.

The enemy knows that when the two of you get serious and come into agreement over your children, they will get off drugs. He knows that when the two of you are in agreement, then nothing is impossible.

But as long as there is bickering and fighting in your house, the enemy will win every time. This is why you have to make up your mind that you are through fighting.

> *But as long as there is bickering and fighting in your house, the enemy will win every time.*

It is time to stop all of the strife and division in your house. If the two of you will come into agreement, you can run the enemy out of your house.

If you are single, then you can find a prayer partner, and run the devil out of your house. If you will make up your mind to gang up on the devil, he won't have a chance. If you'll learn to fight the good fight of faith, then you can be prosperous and build wealth in your family.

"Beloved, how good and pleasant it is for the brethren to dwell together in unity" (Psa. 133:1). It is unity that causes the anointing to flow. If you will come into agreement with your spouse and rebuke the enemy, then there will be a greater anointing than you have known before will fall upon you. There is no telling what God will do if you put down your differences and start agreeing with God.

Even if you do not like each other, begin to rebuke the enemy, come into agreement according to the Word of God, and watch how He will turn your situation around.

When the two of you are in agreement you can take authority over your finances and you will see God work. If the two of you will gang up on your spiritual enemy, then you can deliver a "knockout" punch to him that will turn everything around in your life. It is time to stop fighting each other. It is time to oppose your spiritual enemy in unity.

> *There is no telling what God will do if you put down your differences and start agreeing with God. Even if you do not like each other...*

You need to go ahead and command the blessing on your house in Jesus' Name. The greatest power on earth is when the two of you are in agreement with God.

If you are not walking with your spouse properly today, it is because you are not in agreement with each other and with God. If this is the case, then it is time to get things turned around, if you are going to see your marriage become what it should.

You need to use your faith and call things that "be not as

though they were" (Rom. 4:17). Sometimes you have to treat your spouse as if he or she is wonderful even when you don't believe it. By faith, you have to tell your spouse how lucky you are to have him or her when your mind is telling you the opposite.

It is time to make up your mind to stop fighting each other and begin to fight the good fight of faith. It is time to build up your spouse and to bless your spouse. It is time to get your past behind you. It is time to cleave to each other. This is living in agreement.

10

THE GREEN-EYED MONSTER

Strife does not come just from relationships. It can also come from our own hearts as well. God has a plan for each of us, but if we are not walking in faith and love, then His plan cannot be fulfilled.

If there is jealousy and envy in our hearts, then our lives are not right with God. We need to allow God's plan to operate by giving up some of the dark areas of our hearts that control us far too much.

In the church, we talk a lot about sexual sin, about drunkenness, and about drug abuse, but there is another sin that is every bit as destructive as any of the sins of the flesh. It is the sin of jealousy or envy. James said, "But if you have bitter envy and self-seeking in your hearts, do not boast and lie against the truth. This wisdom does not descend from above, but is earthly, sensual, demonic. For where envy and self-seeking exist, confusion and every evil thing are there" (James 3:14-16).

> *Anytime you are too protective of your territories, it's often a jealousy problem. But now that you are born-again...*

We are all hit with jealousy from time to time, yet people have a difficult time admitting it. So instead of admitting that we are jealous, we say things like, "I'm territorial. I'm not possessive. I'm just protecting what is mine."

But so often the real truth is that we're jealous. Jealousy is a very real problem for many of us.

Anytime you are too protective of your territories, it's often a jealousy problem. But now that you are born-again and seeking to grow up in Christ, you need to learn to overcome the flesh and be more secure in who you are in Christ.

Fear Is The Root Of Jealousy

Jealous people are controlled by fear. They are almost always afraid that someone will take advantage of them, their spouse will cheat on them, or that someone will take away what they already have.

Jealous people are greatly motivated by fear, and their lives are frequently painful and tormented. We need to each examine our own lives by asking ourselves; do we have a difficult time watching other people receive honor, praise, or credit? Does it really burn you when someone else gets the praise and you are unnoticed? What if someone else gets the credit for the things you did? Will jealousy overwhelm you and cause you to flip out or react spitefully?

> ...many times the reason you have difficulties with people is because you are unconsciously jealous of them.

Jealousy can cause you to have problems with other people. In fact, many times the reason you have difficulties with people is because you are unconsciously jealous of them.

However, because of your emotional discomfort, you hide the truth from yourself and try to find fault with them. Since everyone has faults, you can easily blame your internal churning on the person's shortcomings and never have to admit to yourself that you're actually jealous of them. "Well, they think they are something, don't they?" No, they probably do not, but the problem is that you do not think you are something. You are jealous of them, and now you cannot say anything nice about them. The reason you cannot celebrate with others when they have a victory is because you are jealous of them.

Don't kid yourself, if you boil on the inside when others have success, your internal agitation is not caused by concern over their character, but by your personal jealousy.

> ...if you boil on the inside when others have success, your internal agitation is not caused by concern over their character...

Saul had been a great king. He had done a lot for the people, and he was a good leader, but because Saul followed God's instructions somewhat casually, God rejected him as the king of Israel. King Saul never repented of his unbelief but chose instead to guard his kingdom and try to keep others from taking it away.

His fears increased after David killed Goliath because he overheard the women singing, "Saul has slain his thousands, and David his ten thousands" (1 Samuel 18:7).

This infuriated the king and from that moment on, Saul became extremely jealous of David, and it brought about division and turmoil. It was as if the king put on green-tinted glasses. David could have been a great asset to Saul, yet because of his jealousy, Saul put a wrong interpretation on everything David did and always saw David's actions through the eyes of jealousy. Though David was always respectful and humbled himself before Saul, the king was frequently filled with rage and tormented at the thought of David.

This account illustrates the truth that when jealousy comes into your life, everything changes including your demeanor and your attitude.

Once the green-eyed monster has a grip on you, nothing but bitterness comes out of your heart and mouth. At that point, you will lie in order to get what you want or to get even with someone. When people are insecure and fearful, jealousy can easily take over their lives. On the other hand, when you are totally secure with who you are in Christ, you will not be jealous of what others have or what others do.

> *Once the green-eyed monster has a grip on you, nothing but bitterness comes out of your heart and mouth. At that point, you will lie in order to get what you want or to get even with someone.*

The reason you are jealous, then, is because you are insecure. Because of your insecurities, almost anything can make you jealous. Anytime someone tries to take what is yours, it can leave you jealous. When someone tries to move into an area that you have considered your personal domain, you are apt to experience pangs of jealousy and feel threatened. If someone is happy and you are not, this too can leave you jealous.

In fact, jealousy can manifest itself in any realm of your

life in which someone appears to do more, have more, or experience more than you. For example, if you see a husband and a wife who are very caring and affectionate towards each other, it can leave you jealous if you do not have a loving relationship yourself.

> *In fact, jealousy can manifest itself in any realm of your life in which someone appears to do more, have more, or experience more than you.*

Jealousy can cause you to not like others if they have something you wish you had. You can get overlooked on your job and jealousy will rise up. When someone in the choir sings a solo and you do not, it can leave you jealous. Or, you can be good friends with a couple and do lots of things together. Then all of a sudden they may find new friends and drop you. It can hurt you, and jealousy can take root in your life.

Jealous feelings can overtake us anytime we lose something to someone else. This is all about fear of losing control and feelings of insecurity.

RIVALRIES CREATE JEALOUSY

In our society we have a tremendous spirit of competition. We are always comparing ourselves with those around us to see how we measure up, and from this measurement we validate our feelings of success or failure — even though we aren't supposed to compare ourselves with others.

If we see someone extremely successful when we are not, it can create jealousy. When our best friend gets married and leaves us alone, we may start longing for what they have and fall into jealousy again.

> *Competition is a breeding ground for personal dissatisfaction that quickly turns to jealousy as a way to deal with our shortcomings...*

Competition is a breeding ground for personal dissatisfaction that quickly turns to jealousy as a way to deal with our shortcomings — real or imagined. We take anger, greed, and selfishness, wrap it all together and shoot at the backs of others in an attempt to even the score a little more. This can take place in families when one person excels beyond the others. Competition is always dangerous in relationships, even among blood relatives.

Jealousy runs rampant in families when a parent favors one child over another. This is wrong on the parent's part because it can create tremendous feelings of inadequacy.

You may battle with jealousy if your spouse gives too much attention to someone else or is not as loving to you as you need him or her to be.

If your spouse has had an adulterous relationship, and he or she has left you insecure, it can take some time to restore the trust and avoid thoughts of jealousy. It is not so much about forgiving them as it is restoring the trust. Trust has to be earned.

But, sometimes when people are jealous, they question every move that their spouse makes, perhaps because of problems in a past relationship.

> ...when people are jealous, they question every move that their spouse makes, perhaps because of problems in a past relationship.

Jealousy is a serious matter and cannot be ignored. The green-eyed monster is a very ugly emotion and must be dealt with or it will have serious consequences. If your spouse is jealous, you need to sit down and talk about the issues. Find out what is causing the insecurity so the two of you can work on the problem.

If you really love someone, then you do not want your mate to be insecure. You want your mate to feel good about themselves, to be confident, and to live a healthy life. If you really love someone, then you want to find out what your partner's needs are and then make sure those needs are met.

Anytime it appears as if God is blessing others more than He is blessing you, jealousy can rear its ugly head. When we feel cheated in life, jealousy can take hold of us.

If someone accuses you of being jealous, and you immediately take offense and say, "No, I'm not jealous. Not me. I'm not that kind of person." This is usually a cover-up. You need to be able to face yourself and examine your heart.

Often the reason we attack another person's character is that we are jealous. Some people attack their former spouse's reputation because the spouse has gone on with his or her life and they're jealous. The ex is happy, and they can't stand to see her or him happy.

Anytime it appears as though God is blessing others more than He is blessing you, jealousy can rear its ugly head. When we feel cheated in life, the green-eyed monster can take hold of us.

But you must remember, anytime you allow jealousy to come into your life, you will literally stop God's plan for your future. In fact, if you allow jealousy to come into your life, you will stop your destiny, and you will stop the blessings of God.

Miriam was jealous of her brother Moses (Num. 12:1-2). She had saved his life as a child, and now she thought, "Who does he think he is?" She said, "Does God only speak through Moses?" The Bible says that the Lord heard her murmuring, and He allowed her to be sick (Num. 12:9-10).

The problem with Miriam was that she was jealous of her

brother Moses. He was the man with all the power, the authority, and the money. But, instead of rejoicing with him, her jealousy was allowed to run unchecked, and she just had to talk about him. Miriam began to criticize Moses for marrying an Ethiopian woman. Not only was she jealous of Moses because he was in control, she was also prejudiced.

> *The problem with Miriam was that she was jealous of her brother Moses. He was the man with all the power, the authority, and the money.*

The issue here was that Moses had his life together, and Miriam couldn't stand it. Moses was blessed, and Miriam was jealous of his blessings. The truth is that if you allow jealousy to come into your life, you will try to execute someone with your tongue. The Bible says that the religious leaders were jealous of Jesus, and it was because of their jealousy that they wanted Him to die.

PATIENCE DESTROYS JEALOUSY

How do you bear it when people around you are experiencing great success and you are not? How do you endure life when people who are no better than you are experiencing great victories, yet the harder you try, the worse it gets?

Remember, when we become jealous, it is because we are comparing ourselves to other people. God created us to be different. We are not supposed to be the same because we are unique individuals. We are to celebrate our personal and cultural differences. If you compare yourself to other people, you can easily become jealous because a lot of people do things better than you do them.

The Bible says, "And let us not grow weary while doing good, for in due season we shall reap if we do not lose heart" (Gal. 6:9).

If you love the Lord, and you are planting good seed, then you have to believe your time is coming. Even if the money has not come in yet, as long as you are following God's plan for your life, success will eventually come.

> ...when we become jealous, it is because we are comparing ourselves to other people.

Even if the accolades have not come yet, it is only a matter of time. Even if those around you are getting ahead and you are not, you have to believe your time is coming. You have to believe your due season is on the way. You have to believe it is only a matter of time.

It is easier for you to celebrate someone else's victories when you know yours are on the way. But you have to be patient in the kingdom of God. If you are not patient, then jealousy will overtake you, and it will create many broken relationships and a miserable life.

Patience will always destroy jealousy because all that jealousy really is, is an attitude that says, "I want what is mine right now." You can praise God and celebrate someone else's victories and successes without being jealous when you know your season is coming.

> It is easier for you to celebrate someone else's victories when you know yours are on the way.

The Lord wants us to have so much faith in Him that we don't go by what we see. Even when others are promoted ahead of us, we have to believe that our day is coming.

When you are serving the Lord, you do not have to worry about your future because "The steps of a good man are ordered by the Lord" (Psa. 37:23). So stop being jealous of others and snap out of it. Your blessings may have been delayed, but they cannot be stopped.

Because you are diligently seeking the Lord and putting Him first, it is only a matter of time until His blessings come. When God says that it is someone's season, no devil in hell can stop the breakthrough.

You have got to tell yourself, "My day is coming. I will

not give up. I am not going to be broke forever. It is only a matter of time until God brings me into my season of fruitfulness."

It does not matter if you are so broke that you cannot rub two nickels together. If you will be faithful to the Lord, then your day will come. This is why it is foolish for you to be jealous of anything that other people have.

You cannot covet anything that belongs to someone else or God will not be pleased with you. Besides it is crazy to be jealous of someone because you do not know the price that they paid to get where they are.

Everybody pays a price to get where they are. Anytime you see a great business, a great family, or a great ministry, you can bet someone paid a price to get there. Anytime you see someone head up a great children's department or a great music department, you can bet someone paid the price and went through a lot of pain to get there. The higher you go, the greater the price.

Do not ever be jealous of what other people have unless you are willing to pay the price they paid. Anytime you cannot rejoice with your brothers and sisters when they are getting ahead of you, you can bet that jealousy is the reason.

If you have a hard time complimenting others, then there's a good chance that you struggle with jealousy issues. This is why you need to learn to give genuine compliments every chance you have.

Every time someone you know gets blessed, learn to celebrate. Learn to applaud their blessings, and rejoice with them. Learn to give compliments liberally. Tell them how happy you are for them, and how proud you are of them.

> *Do not ever be jealous of what other people have unless you are willing to pay the price they paid.*

If others around you are being blessed and you're not, just remember that if you are obeying the Word of God, it is only a matter of time until He commands the blessing on you. It is only a matter of time until you are blessed coming in and blessed going out.

Because you are planting good seed, you should not lose heart in doing good. God will bring your breakthrough to pass. In the meantime, stop talking about other people and begin rejoicing with them about their success.

You cannot afford to be jealous. You need blessings and miracles in your life, but jealousy will rob them from you. It will also steal your peace and your joy. If reading this causes you to be uncomfortable, it is probably because it has touched a sensitive area in your life.

You need to say, "Lord, I give You all of my pain. I ask You to bring healing into my life." It is time to grow up in Christ and destroy the jealousy that is destroying you, and harming others, by patiently following God's plan for your life.

BABY, YOU ARE SO FINE

11

CONCERNING DIVORCE AND REMARRIAGE

In the book of Genesis, we are told that God created Adam and Eve (Gen. 1-2). It was God's way of saying that He made one man for one woman. Then He told them to be fruitful and to multiply. The Lord also told us that a man should leave his father and his mother and cleave to his wife. In other words, when a couple marries, they should have enough going for them that they don't have to depend on their parents for support.

Therefore, one key to a Godly marriage is for one man and one woman to work together to create a family for God.

God also said that "they shall become one flesh" (Gen. 2:24). The marriage covenant is not the same thing as shacking up together or as a common-law agreement. The Biblical marriage covenant requires that you make vows of responsibility for each other before God and before men because in a Biblical marriage two separate lives are becoming one.

There is something spiritual that takes place in a marriage covenant that does not happen in any other living arrangement. The "oneness" that happens between a couple is to be similar to the "Oneness" of the Trinity in heaven. Therefore, the marriage is to be a spiritual bonding governed by love from Almighty God.

> There is something spiritual that takes place in a marriage covenant that does not happen in any other living arrangement.

God also says that no man should separate those whom He joins together in marriage. If you know people who are married, then you should be very careful about offering them unmerited or ungodly advice; "I wouldn't put up with that. I would divorce them in a minute."

If you are experiencing marital problems today, you should be careful about listening to other people's advice. Be very careful about telling people your struggles, and be careful of the advice that you receive. Remember that Eve began to listen to voices other than her husband's, and she got into trouble. It is God's will that you learn to trust in Him. God never goes against His Word.

You may be giving your spouse and children the love and support they need, but that love and support may not be returned to you.

Even as a Christian, you can reach a point where you feel you cannot go any further. It may seem that the only way to keep your sanity is to allow your spouse and your children to go their desired direction, and you go yours.

However, before you do this you need to get into God's Word and find out what He says about divorce. You need to pray about it and put your situation into God's hands and trust Him to help you.

> *It is God's will that you learn to trust in Him. God never goes against His Word.*

WHY GOD HATES DIVORCE

When Jesus was telling His disciples that God hated divorce, they spoke up and asked, "If God hates divorce, why did He allow divorce through Moses?" (Mark 10:2-9). Jesus answered and said that Moses permitted divorce because of abusive relationships, an inability or refusal to forgive, and other "heavy baggage" from the past that prevented the establishment of a healthy marriage.

So rather than allow two people to torment each other endlessly, God permitted divorce. But He was careful to say that their hearts were hardened in these situations.

> When two people meet, they are both carrying huge packs on their backs full of stuff from their past.

When two people meet, they are both carrying huge packs on their backs full of stuff from their past. The problem with this baggage is that while you can see what other people are carrying, it is hard to see your own stack behind you. It is this excess baggage that causes broken hearts and relationships, and eventually brings people to the divorce courts.

The reason a man cannot love his wife the way Jesus loved the church is because of the baggage in his past. The reason a woman cannot submit to her husband is because of the baggage in her past. Here are some examples from your backpack of baggage, behaviors and attitudes that get in the way of healthy, whole relationships: (1) nobody can tell you anything, you can't take criticism even though you are pretty good at giving it out; (2) you are attracted to people who treat you like a dog, your low self-esteem causes you to choose partners who put you down so you can't fight back for your dignity; and (3) you have gone from one relationship to another and none of your partners have felt secure with you, you are never satisfied with what you have and are always looking for something or someone better.

We must face the facts, and realize that people go through divorces because of the baggage from their past.

As Jesus was talking with His disciples, He made a very controversial statement. He said, "Whoever divorces his wife, except for sexual immorality, and marries another, commits adultery; and whoever marries her who is divorced commits adultery" (Matt. 19:9).

He said that God permits divorce, but turned right around and said that if you remarry, you are committing adultery. This seems to be a contradiction. How could God permit divorce and then condemn people to living single for the rest of their lives? Isn't God supposed to be in the restoring and forgiving business? Doesn't God give us another chance if we fail, and doesn't He love us no matter what?

To truly understand Jesus' statement and the disciples' shock, you have to go back to the Jewish or Mosaic Law and look at what society was like under this law. Even during Jesus' life, the children of Israel were under the Law. And, under the Mosaic Law, they could divorce and they could remarry at will. A good Jew would never commit adultery. But, under the

Law, he could marry someone this week, and when he got tired of her, simply divorce her. Under the Law, this was legal.

In other words, the popular interpretation of this portion of the Law by the children of Israel was that they could have sex with whomever they wanted as long as the partners were married to each other at the time. In other words, they could have serial marriages, one after the other, but they were not permitted to have sex outside of marriage.

> The reason a man cannot love his wife the way Jesus loved the church is because of the baggage in his past. The reason a woman cannot submit to her husband is because of the baggage in her past.

So, when they tired of each other, they just simply divorced. Jesus said that in behaving this way, they were nothing more than adulterers because their hearts were not right and they had twisted the purpose of the Law. Contrary to their thinking, Jesus said that whoever divorces his wife, except for immorality in the marriage, is living in sin.

Paul set the record straight for the New Covenant. He said that if you are married, you are not to seek a divorce. He went on to say that if you are born-again and your unbelieving spouse leaves you, then you are no longer tied to him or her. If you remarry after an unbelieving spouse leaves, then you have not sinned (1 Cor. 7:28).

To simplify and summarize Paul's statements here, he is saying the following: If you have sex before marriage, then you have sinned. If you have sex after a divorce and it is before remarriage, then you have sinned. But if you remarry, you have not sinned. As Paul says, "it is better to marry than to burn (with passion)" (1 Cor. 7:9).

God hates divorce because of the way it hurts people and tears them apart. He hates the way it divides families and destroys households.

> *God hates divorce because of the way it hurts people and tears them apart.*

When you go through a divorce, you experience an incredible amount of pain. This is because there is tremendous protection in marriage, even if it is not a great one and when this protection is removed, there is pain.

It is not my intention to preach against divorce. It is my goal to tell you what God wants in a Godly marriage. The Bible says that marriage is supposed to be a lifetime commitment (1 Cor. 7:27).

But the Bible also shows that our sin nature does bring failure. Divorce can be one of the most life-crushing experiences one can go through. It can be devastating and even dehumanizing.

It creates tremendous pain and the ripple effect of that pain reaches far outside the immediate family. Its effects can extend several generations. For these reasons and more, God hates divorce.

On the other hand, we must remember that we live in a fallen world, and we are all fallen creatures. The church needs to recognize that some Christian marriages are going to end in divorce because of the sin nature in man. As the church of Jesus Christ, we must learn to respond in God's love. God hates divorce, but He loves His people. God's love says that if you find yourself divorced, Jesus came to heal your broken heart.

> Divorce can be one of the most life-crushing experiences one can go through. It can be devastating and even dehumanizing.

It says that He came to heal the rejected, the broken, and the downtrodden, and if you find yourself in a hurting marriage, that certainly applies to you. We also need to recognize that divorce does not have as much to do with the courthouse as it does with our sin nature. It has to do with our selfishness and with our self-centeredness.

Great marriages take place when two people are determined to meet each other's needs. But we are selfish by nature, and tend to put our wants ahead of the other person's needs. If we obeyed the Word of God, we would be very careful about getting into marriage to begin with.

DIVORCE IS NOT THE END

> *Great marriages take place when two people are determined to meet each other's needs.*

If you are having trouble in your marriage, it is God's will that you forgive each other and not get a divorce. But, if you find yourself divorced, you must know that God wants to help you.

There is life afterward and "if you confess your sins, He is faithful and just to forgive you and cleanse you from all unrighteousness" (1 John 1:9). God is not mad at you, and He wants to restore your life.

You need to know that with God, divorce is not the end of your relationship with Him. In fact, when you love the Lord, the death of your marriage is always the beginning of something new. Divorce is never God's best, but God takes what the enemy meant to destroy you and turns it for your good. This point can never be repeated too much, and it applies to every failure and mistake in your life.

Even though divorce is a tremendous failure for a Christian to experience, God has a way of changing you through it all. He even has a way of turning it for your good. Unfortunately,

Christian marriages fail because Christians fail. It is a fact of life. "We have all sinned and fell short of the glory of God" (Rom. 3:23).

Even though divorce is a tremendous failure for a Christian to experience, God has a way of changing you through it all.

If Jesus is our model, then we should oppose divorce and try to bring healing into troubled marriages, but once divorce has taken place, clearly we must extend love, compassion, and forgiveness to those involved. This position shouldn't be that difficult to understand. For example, we open our arms to drug addicts and to alcoholics, so shouldn't we open our arms to divorced people who have failed?

We tell convicts, even murderers, that Jesus loves them and that He will forgive them. Shouldn't we treat divorced people the same way? It is interesting how Jesus forgave the woman caught in adultery (John 8:3-11), yet some church folks cannot seem to forgive those who are divorced. They seem to have sterner standards than what God has.

The gospel is about forgiveness and restoration, in fact, that is the whole point of the gospel. It is not God's will for divorce to take place. But the purpose of the gospel is to give people another chance, and allow them to start over.

If your gospel does not lift people out of their mess, it isn't much good. If the gospel you preach doesn't bring people together in love, then it is not the gospel of Jesus Christ.

Why do some believe that God will forgive any sin yet teach that divorce is unforgivable? Jesus forgave the woman at the well, who had been married five times (John 4:1-42). Should we not do the same?

Paul said, "For I am persuaded that neither death nor life, nor angels, nor principalities, nor powers, nor things present, nor things to come, nor height, nor depth, nor any other created thing, shall be able to separate us from the love of God which is in Jesus Christ" (Rom. 8:38-39).

> *The gospel is about forgiveness and restoration, in fact, that is the whole point of the gospel.*

You need to know that if you find yourself divorced, it is not God's will, but neither is it the unpardonable sin. There is only one unpardonable sin and that is to reject Jesus Christ as Lord and Savior. There is life after divorce. If you will go to God and give Him the broken pieces of your life, He will put you back together again.

Perhaps you are still married and your spouse is not saved, and you find it difficult to continue in the relationship. God says that if you are married to an unbeliever stay if you can.

Even if it is only for the children's sake, it is better to stay.

But if the unbeliever wants to leave, then let him or her go. If the unbeliever is willing to live with you and willing for you to serve the Lord, then stay. If your mate is agreeable for you to raise the children in the ways of the Lord, then stay. Do not seek to be released. Now if you are married to a believer, then you are to never seek to be released in the marriage. If they leave, they leave, but your stand should be one of believing God.

> There is life after divorce. If you will go to God and give Him the broken pieces of your life, He will put you back together again.

Perhaps you are married to a believer and you know your spouse has been unfaithful, and you are wondering what you should do. Paul said that you have a choice (1 Cor. 7).

God's will is that you forgive each other and allow the Lord to heal the broken areas. But, when that is not possible, God allows divorce.

Perhaps you are divorced and someone told you that if you remarry you would be living in sin for the rest of your life. Paul said that if you remarry, you have not sinned (1 Cor. 7:28). But, if you are divorced, do not seek for a husband or for a wife. If you seek for a husband (or wife), you might find trouble. "But seek first the kingdom of God and His righteousness, and all these things shall be added to you" (Matt. 6:33). While you are single, use this time to work on the baggage of your past. Then in due season, allow God to bring someone into your life.

If you are divorced today, make up your mind not to repeat the same mistakes you made in the past. If you are attracted to people who are not good for you, make up your mind that you are not going in that direction again. Only a fool would go out with the same kind of people and expect different results.

If you are single today, then you need to use your faith in the Lord to bring you someone who loves God more than you.

If this is going to be your year, then you have to make some changes starting today. If this is going to be your year for a turnaround, then you have to do things differently. If this is going to be your year, then you have to forgive, forget, and let things go.

12

FROM THIS DAY FORWARD

Do you remember your wedding day? Everything had to be just right. The invitations had been sent, the preparations had been made, and the flowers were perfect. The bridesmaids, the groomsmen, the rings, and the reception hall were all ready for the wedding. Everyone was nervous.

It was the most important day of your life. You had waited to get married because you were determined to wait for the right person. When you finally married, it was for life.

On the day you married, you made a lot of promises and a lot of vows. You promised to love, to honor, and to cherish one another. You promised to be help-meets to each other. You said, "I will love you no matter what; till death do us part, and as long as we both shall live."

In your wedding vows you said, "I will love you no matter what. I will stay with you in sickness and in health and for richer or for poorer. I will forsake all others. I promise to cleave to you and to no one else."

Unrealistic Expectations

> What happened between that wonderful day and where you are right now? What has caused the two of you to be at each other's throats...

What happened between that wonderful day and where you are right now? What has caused the two of you to be at each other's throats, or caused you to not trust each other, or caused you to sleep in the same bed, but to not touch anymore? What has caused you to be sharp and critical with your words?

There was a day when you thought you couldn't live without each other. There was a day when you wanted to spend the rest of your life with that person. But today, you cannot imagine spending one more day with him or her. What baggage has entered into your marriage, and why are you fantasizing about someone else you have just met? Why are you secretly holding on to the memories of other people from your past, and wishing you were still there? Aren't you supposed to take every thought captive to the obedience of Jesus Christ and pull down every stronghold (2 Cor. 10:4-5)?

Marriage is not easy. It requires hard work in order to make it succeed. Unless you put the Lord first and lean on Him together, your marriage will probably fail.

The Bible says that when any two agree about anything, it shall be done for them (Matt. 18:19 paraphrased). It seems as though couples are not touching, so they are not agreeing. There was a time when you could not keep your hands off of each other, but today you are not even touching. Something inside of you has changed since the day you were married.

> *There was a time when you could not keep your hands off of each other, but today you are not even touching.*

We have unrealistic expectations when it comes to marriage. There is something inside each of us that does not actually believe we will have to put our vows to the test. We think that all we have to do is fall in love and we'll live happily ever after. Our problem is that we make all of these promises on our wedding day, but we don't understand the longevity of the vows. Today, while everything is great, we believe what we say, but our faith and our vows are truly tested when the storms hit.

It is unrealistic to think that there will not be problems in a relationship. It is unrealistic to think there will never be arguments or disagreements. It is unrealistic to think any person can meet all our needs.

> Our marriage partners are supposed to be helpers, but only Jesus can meet all of our needs. Only Jesus can fill the voids...

Our marriage partners are supposed to be helpers, but only Jesus can meet all of our needs. Only Jesus can fill the voids, only Jesus can meet the needs, and only Jesus can help you.

After you have been married to someone for a while, you let your guard down. Once you do this, you will see the worst in each other. It will just come out. In a marriage relationship you must be willing to change if you expect to have a happy life. You must be willing to make adjustments, and you must be willing not to have your own way, at least some of the time.

Because of all the baggage of the past, many married couples have separate bank accounts because they do not trust each other. Aren't you supposed to be one flesh? Isn't it "till death do you part," or is it, "until the money runs out"? It is God's desire to bring the two of you together in such a way that you really do become one.

What Are You Saying About Your Spouse

It is interesting that Adam gave Eve her name. He first called her woman (Gen. 2:23). Then he called her Eve (Gen. 3:20). She became what he called her. Husbands, what do you call your wives?

Do you call her baby doll or do you call her stupid? Do you call her sweet thing or do you call her ugly? Do you call her the apple of your eye or do you call her fat? The Bible says, "death and life are in the power of the tongue" (Prov. 18:21).

> *Do you call her baby doll or do you call her stupid? Do you call her sweet thing or do you call her ugly? Do you call her the apple of your eye or do you call her fat?*

The words you speak to one another will definitely affect your attitude toward each other. Some of you need to change your words right now.

Sometimes you have to speak words of encouragement to your spouse by faith. The Bible says we are to call things that be not as though they were (Rom. 4:17). In other words, even though your spouse is not what you want, you must speak faith to your spouse.

Paul said that every man is supposed to wash his wife in the water of the Word that he might present her to himself in

181

all her glory (Eph. 5:26). She will become whatever you call her.

Husband, are you washing your wife in the water of the Word? If you will brag on her, she will rise to the occasion, and she will do everything possible to live up to what you are saying. You need to understand that you are one flesh (Gen. 2:24). If you nurture your spouse, you are nurturing yourself. If you bless your spouse, you are blessing yourself. To paraphrase Genesis 2:23 and Ephesians 5:28-29 liberally, "Baby, you are bone of my bone and flesh of my flesh, and if I love you, I love myself."

> You have to make up your mind to forget the things of the past and to say that it is a new day.

You have to make up your mind to forget the things of the past and to say that it is a new day. In other words, from this day forward, you are going to nurture and encourage each other. From this day forward, you are going to stop criticizing and start building one another up.

If you will build up your spouse properly, he or she will never go looking for approval from someone else.

Eve began to listen to other voices besides her husband's, and she got into trouble. You need to be careful about standing around the water cooler and telling people how bad your spouse is.

Be careful about picking up the phone and calling your friends and telling them about your marriage problems. Be careful to whom you talk, and be careful what you say.

Similarly women, if you really love your husband, you should never allow anybody to talk negatively about him. Men, you should never allow anybody to talk negatively or disrespectfully about your wife because she is a part of you, and to do so is to show disrespect toward yourself.

Many marriages have been destroyed because somebody was listening to the wrong voices. It is amazing how many messes we get ourselves into because we listen to our friends rather than obeying God's Word.

> Eve began to listen to other voices besides her husband's, and she got into trouble. You need to be careful about standing around the water cooler and telling people how bad your spouse is.

God intends for the man to be the protector of his wife and of the home. In fact, the man is supposed to be a covering for his wife. She is supposed to know that she is safe with him.

When a husband is truly a covering over his wife, he is the one who sleeps closest to the door in case there is trouble. When they walk down the street, he is the one who walks on the side where trouble could arise.

A Godly man loves his wife as Christ loved the church (Eph. 5:25). A Godly woman is a praying woman. Her primary concern must be to pray for her husband and cover him in prayer every day.

If your marriage is a mess today, it is not too late to turn it around. The devil has come "to kill, to steal and to destroy" (John 10:10). You have to be determined that he is not going to win.

> When a husband is truly a covering over his wife, he is the one who sleeps closest to the door in case there is trouble. When they walk down the street, he is the one who walks on the side where trouble could arise.

You need to say today, "From this day forward it's just you and me, baby. Forsaking all others I will cleave only to you." Husband, you cannot be running with the fellas while your wife is at home taking care of the kids. You are to forsake all others and cleave to each other.

It may not be easy to follow God's Word, but it is always the best course to take. You have been hurt in the past, but it is time to put it behind you and start trusting God. You cannot change what people have done to you, but you can be released from the pain if you will truly forgive, from this day forward.

It is time to release all of the grudges. Lord, "forgive us our debts as we forgive our debtors" (Matt. 6:12). God wants you to drop the charges you have against one another. It is time to cancel the debt your mate owes you and issue a statement of forgiveness.

If there is going to be a turnaround in your life, then you have to drop the charges. You need to touch and agree with each other. You need to believe that the past is the past and what is done is done. You need to believe that, with God's help and His guidance, everything is going to change from this day forward.

> *God wants you to drop the charges you have against one another. It is time to cancel the debt your mate owes you and issue a statement of forgiveness.*

May I suggest that you sit down with your spouse and read the following words together, in unison, as one means of getting a fresh start in your marriage today:

"From this day forward we are not going to talk about the things we have done to each other. We are not going to talk about the hurts in our relationship."

"From this day forward, we are going to put away the past and press on to a new future. From this day forward we will not allow insecurity to rule us, and we will not allow jealousy to hurt our relationship."

"From this day forward we will nurture and build up each other. From this day forward we will do everything within our power to meet each other's needs and to love each other the way we need to be loved."

"From this day forward, we are determined to get back to our wedding vows and obey God's Word."

CONCLUSION

I hope that reading "Baby, You Are So Fine" has caused you to examine your own life. I hope that this book has benefited you and brought healing to your life.

I want to encourage you to keep working at your relationships; with God, your spouse, your children, your family, friends and co-workers. Relationships take time to build and hurts take time to heal, but God's Word tells us that those who wait upon the Lord shall renew their strength.

If you are looking for more resources to help you in your walk with the Lord, I have many materials that can help you. Some of the materials are listed on the following pages and I can send you a catalog that will give you more information

that will help you and more information about Dennis Leonard
Ministries or you can visit my website.

Remember, your best days are still ahead!

Bishop Dennis Leonard
9495 East Florida Avenue
Denver, Colorado 80231
(303) 369-8514
Monday - Friday 8:30 - 4:30 PM MST
www.bishopdennisleonard.com

ABOUT THE AUTHOR

Bishop Dennis Leonard is the Pastor and Founder of Heritage Christian Center in Denver, Colorado, which is recognized as one of the most successful churches in America. Heritage Christian Center serves over 12,000 people in weekly attendance.

Perhaps Bishop Leonard's greatest achievement has been his ability to attract and retain one of the most ethnically diverse congregations in America. He has accomplished at Heritage Christian Center what many churches from different denominations have found almost impossible to achieve – it has broken down racial, denominational, social and economic barriers and has successfully bridged that gap between these different ethnic groups, forging different cultural and economic interests into one cohesive, loving unit.

Bishop Leonard has been described by his peers, and the greater secular and spiritual community, as a true leader and an example to follow in the Ministry of Reconciliation between races and denominations.

He is a visionary and answers the call of missions both overseas and here in the United States. It is his firm belief that the church must be mobilized almost as if it were an army to do the work of the ministry.

One of Bishop Leonard's most outstanding success stories is the establishment of a widespread prison outreach. The Heritage Christian Center Prison Ministry literally receives countless numbers of letters weekly from incarcerated men and women nationwide. The Prison Ministry Team consistently visits one or more prisons every day throughout the state of Colorado and the neighboring region. In 1997, Bishop Leonard, with the congregation of Heritage Christian Center supporting his vision, purchased and installed satellite dishes in every prison in the state of Colorado in order to meet the desperate need for Christian television within the prison walls.

Bishop Leonard looks for every opportunity possible to preach the Gospel and minister to the lost. As a result of this effort to find avenues for the ministry, he believes that national television is a critical importance to his mission and the mission of Heritage Christian Center.

He currently airs his weekly television program, *"Touching a Hurting World"* on the Black Entertainment Network (BET). This program reaches hundreds of thousands of television households all over the United States in virtually every major city in America, in addition, Bishop Leonard airs two times weekly on the Trinity Broadcasting Network on the Denver, Colorado affiliate.

Bishop Leonard has established a new project at Heritage Christian Center called, "Project Heritage". The mission of Project Heritage is to reach outside the four walls of the church and into the community in order to touch the lives of people where they are hurting. Project Heritage provides housing, job-training, counseling and childcare to families who are trying to rebuild their lives.

And finally, in September 1999, Bishop Leonard was consecrated Bishop of Multi-Cultural Ministries in the Full Gospel Baptist Church Fellowship. Bishop Leonard is the first white man to be consecrated as Bishop with the Full Gospel Baptist Church Fellowship headed by International Presiding Bishop, Bishop Paul S. Morton, Sr.. This new task at hand will open the doors for Bishop Leonard to spread the vision that God gave him several years ago, "It's not a black thing, it's not a white thing, it's a Jesus thing." The multi-cultural ministry that God began and established at Heritage Christian Center can now be taken to the world.

Do You Want To Receive Jesus Christ as Your Lord and Savior?

The Bible says, *"That if thou shalt confess with thy mouth the Lord Jesus, and shalt believe in thine heart that God raised him from the dead, thou shalt be saved. For with the heart man believeth unto righteousness; and with the mouth confession is made unto salvation"* [Romans 10:9,10].
If you want to receive Jesus Christ as the Lord and Savior of your life, sincerely pray the prayer below from your heart;

Jesus, I believe that You died for me and that You rose from the dead. I confess to You that I am a sinner and that I need your forgiveness. Forgive me Lord of my sins and cleanse me from my unrighteousness. Come into my life and give me eternal life. I confess You now as my Lord and my Savior. Begin today to make me the person that I need to be. Put in me those things that need to be in me and remove those things that need to come out. Thank you for dying on the cross for me.
In Jesus' name, Amen!

Signed _____ Date _____

Name _____

Address _____

City _____ State _____ Zip _____

Phone (h) _____

E-mail: _____

Write To Us:
We want to hear from you and we would like to send you information that will help you with your new walk with the Lord.
Dennis Leonard Ministries
9495 East Florida Avenue • Denver, CO 80231 • 303-369-8514
www.bishopdennisleonard.com

MY PERSONAL NOTES

MY PERSONAL NOTES

BABY, YOU ARE SO FINE

MY PERSONAL NOTES

BABY, YOU ARE SO FINE

MY PERSONAL NOTES

MY PERSONAL NOTES

BABY, YOU ARE SO FINE

MY PERSONAL NOTES

MY PERSONAL NOTES

BABY, YOU ARE SO FINE

MY PERSONAL NOTES

MY PERSONAL NOTES

BABY, YOU ARE SO FINE

MY PERSONAL NOTES

BABY, YOU ARE SO FINE

MY PERSONAL NOTES

BABY, YOU ARE SO FINE

MY PERSONAL NOTES

BABY, YOU ARE SO FINE

MY PERSONAL NOTES

_____

_____

_____

_____

_____

_____

_____

_____

_____

_____

_____

_____

_____

_____

_____

_____

_____

_____

_____

_____

_____

_____

BABY, YOU ARE SO FINE

MY PERSONAL NOTES

BABY, YOU ARE SO FINE

MY PERSONAL NOTES

BABY, YOU ARE SO FINE